Coping with Overwhelming Grief

When
Death
Isn't Fair

Joy Swift

REVIEW AND HERALD® PUBLISHING ASSOCIATION
HAGERSTOWN, MD 21740

The author assumes full responsibility for the accuracy of all facts
and quotations as cited in this book.

Texts credited to NIV are from the *Holy Bible, New International
Version.* Copyright © 1973, 1978, 1984, International Bible
Society. Used by permission of Zondervan Bible Publishers.

This book was
Edited by Gerald Wheeler
Copyedited by Jocelyn Fay and James Cavil
Cover designed by Mark O'Conner
Interior designed by Tina M. Ivany
Cover photo by The Image Bank
Electronic makeup by Shirley M. Bolivar
Typeset: Bembo 11/13

PRINTED IN U.S.A.

05 04 03 02 01   5 4 3 2 1

R&H Cataloging Service
Swift, Joy, 1957-
    When death isn't fair: coping with overwhelming grief.

    1. Grief.   I. Title.

                152.4

ISBN 0-8280-1694-1

Also by Joy Swift:
        Goodbye Forever?

To order, call 1-800-765-6955.
Visit us at www.reviewandherald.com for information on
other Review and Herald products.

I dedicate this book
to the memory of those who lost their
lives to the terrorist attacks of
September 11, 2001.
May these pages bring comfort and
healing to those who are left to endure
life without them.
My heart goes out to each
and every one of you.

Joy

Contents

ONE

Attack on America

I expected September 11 to be a little different from the average day. It had been so for 28 years now. I lingered a little longer with my husband, reluctant to leave him on our wedding anniversary, knowing full well that this happy date would be overshadowed by the anniversary of the deaths of our five children just four days from now. Incredible how two anniversaries only days apart can create such vastly different memories. But both dates reminded us that no matter what happened we would love each other forever.

My heart told me to stay right there in my husband's arms, for this was my favorite place to be, and I needed the extra comfort to bolster myself against the anniversary of loss. My job at the hardware store, however, demanded that I get out of bed and meet my eight-hour obligation. I had barely raised my head from the pillow when the phone rang. It was our daughter Sandy.

"Do you know what's going on?" she said in disbelief. "They just flew a plane into the World Trade Center!"

George raced to the television and flipped it on. We sat, stunned, as the horrible news played across the screen, having barely digested the impact of the first plane when a second banked sharply and plowed through the second tower right before our eyes. When our hearts felt they could take no more, scenes from the Pentagon forced us deeper into shock.

And then the towers fell, sending rescuers and onlookers fleeing for their very lives. Finally came word of a fourth plane crashing violently in Pennsylvania, leaving a huge crater in the earth and tearing an equally huge crater into the hearts of Americans nationwide.

This could not be happening. Not to America. Not today.

Customers who came to the hardware store seemed to be in a stupor, unable to fully concentrate, needing to talk about what was happening, repeating what they had heard on television, trying to make sense of the tragedy. But it was too much for our hearts to comprehend all at once.

Over the next few days I listened as people compared the week's events to Pearl Harbor, Oklahoma City, the California earthquake, and the Korean War. But it was nothing like anything we'd ever encountered before. Like everybody else, I searched my memory for something in my past that might offer the coping skills I now needed to make sense of this day.

As I watched all those survivors standing outside the rubble, clinging to photos of their loved ones missing since the buildings collapsed, my soul cried out to every one of them. The men and women simply would not leave—they would stand vigil and wait no matter how long. Police lines kept them at a distance and denied them access to where their loved ones might be lying at this very moment, but they would not depart.

Thousands lined the litter-strewn sidewalks, clinging to some shred of hope that their loved one somehow had made it out alive. They could not yet focus on the inevitable. It was too early to give up hope.

For days the rescue mission continued as multitudes gathered from around the world to offer any assistance they could. America united as never before in support of the victims. Flag manufacturers could not possibly meet the demand as citizens rushed to fly the colors of freedom. Eighty nations from around the globe recognized the sobering reality that some of their citizens had been in the towers that fatal morning.

Rescuers continued to sift through the rubble, hour by excruciating hour, as the list of those missing grew into the thousands. With each bucketful the unspoken cry rang loud and clear: "We are America! And we will not take this lying down."

"By aiding and abetting murder, the Taliban regime is committing murder," President George W. Bush declared in his address to the country. "Whether we bring our enemies to justice or bring justice to our enemies, justice will be done. . . . Every nation in every region now has a decision to make: Either you are with us or you are with the terrorists. . . . Any nation that continues to harbor or support terrorism will be regarded by the United States as a hostile regime."

As time wore on, hopes that air pockets might

still shelter victims grew fainter until no hope remained. The real grieving began then as shock gave way to reality.

I lay awake night after night, hearing their cries as clearly as I had heard my own so many years before: *He was so caring. . . . She was so beautiful. . . . They were so young. . . . They never hurt anybody. They didn't deserve to die! Why did this happen, God? Don't You understand how precious this one was to me? This whole thing is so senseless. What did they gain by killing the innocent? I'm trying so hard to be strong, God, but I just can't be. Bring them back, God! Please, bring them back!*

As the voices echoed in my brain I thought of all the people God had put in my path to ease my suffering and to guide me gently to the answers I so desperately needed. The nurse who cried with me in the hospital and showed me from the Bible that Jesus was coming soon to take us home. The mother who let me hold her baby as long as I wanted to after she learned that my own had been killed. The funeral home employee who told me to do what was in my heart. The pastor who challenged me to make him prove every answer from the Bible, and then opened the plan of salvation to my aching heart.

How I longed to comfort the survivors, each one my brother, my sister in Christ. How I longed to get in *their* path and assure them that there are answers to their deepest questions, that there *is* healing after the valley of the shadow of death. That there *is* light where we now see darkness. That there *is* justice for the innocent. And that there *is* hope beyond today.

And so I write this book in the hope that it will

help the multitude who mourn their incredible loss, one precious loved one at a time. May these pages provide the comfort, support, and answers each of them so desperately need.

TWO

When Tragedy Struck Twice

I t was in the fifth game that the stranger called us out of the American Legion Bingo Hall to tell us that "something terrible" had happened. "Please, just go home," he cried as he turned away to hide the tears coursing down his cheeks.

A sense of urgency gripped us as we sped for home, where we had left our four youngest children alone for the evening. A million tragedies played through our minds, wondering what terrible thing awaited our arrival.

Visible even three miles away, the flashing red emergency lights pierced the night sky above our house. The roadblock barely slowed my husband down as he barreled on through and rounded the last bend. Patrol cars and ambulances lined both sides of the road.

George leaped from the car and bolted for the front door only to have two police officers on the porch stop him. One of them pulled a gun on him.

Two ambulance attendants grabbed me by the arms as I tried to keep up with him.

"Let me go!" I screamed at them. "Those are my kids in there!"

They pulled me across the road to the rear of an ambulance and sat me down on the bumper. I turned to see George still struggling with the officers on the porch. They clearly weren't going to let him inside.

"Where are my kids?" I asked the attendants who stood guard over me. "Are they in the ambulance?" I whirled to look inside, but the gurneys were empty.

The woman's eyes met mine. "They're still in the house," she murmured.

I strained to look across the road to my living room window. But beyond the pulsating red glow, the house lay still and black. My mind reeled with questions. Why won't they let us inside? If the kids are hurt, why isn't somebody in there helping them? But if they're OK, why won't they let them come out to us?

I sat on the bumper, trying to be rational, trying to figure out what was happening. All at once it hit me. I turned to search the woman's eyes.

"They're all dead, aren't they?" I said.

The male attendant kicked a stone with his shoe. The woman nodded her head and whispered, "Yes."

The physical pain of that moment felt as if something had ripped my heart out of my chest.

The authorities would tell us only that the children had been shot. As George stood in shock, I threw myself into a rage, babbling and carrying on, trying to turn back the clock, to change the past few hours, to save my children's lives.

The authorities took us to the police station, immediately separated us, and held us for 10 hours of interrogations, strip searches, and powder-residue tests. We were suspects in the murders of our own children. It was an intensely angry night for me, the rage and disbelief bolstering my strength to superhuman proportions.

The following morning, with no evidence to hold us, the police released us with orders not to leave town. That night they took the real killers into custody. The murderer was a 14-year-old boy who had played with our son, Greg. His accomplice, 20-year-old Ray Richardson, Jr., didn't even know the children's names.

We learned through police that Billy Dyer had bragged repeatedly during a two-week period about his plan to steal guns from our house and that he would not hesitate to kill anyone who got in his way. Later the authorities revealed that Billy had a juvenile record in two states and had attempted murder before. He had planned to use the guns to go on a killing spree until he got caught.

Five days later we buried our children by order of age: Steven, 14; Gregory, 12; Tonya, 3; and Stacy, 17 months. But the tragedy was not yet over.

Our oldest daughter, Stephanie, 17, lay in a hospital bed the night Billy had gunned down her brothers and sisters. Twenty days later her six-week-long battle with cancer ended, and we laid her to rest beside the other four. Within a span of three weeks our family of seven had diminished to just George and me. Enormous grief engulfed the days and weeks that followed.

Though the state charged both defendants with four counts of capital murder, the 14-year-old pleaded guilty to a lesser charge and is currently serving two life sentences. His accomplice also received a reduced sentence and served just six and a half years before being paroled. He later committed suicide. Billy remains a part of our lives, since he is entitled to parole hearings every two years. Each hearing reopens the wound as we fight passionately to keep him behind bars.

Many years have passed since we buried our children. George and I have weathered the horrendous storm together. Since then we have had three more children, now all grown and on their own. We've recovered as best we can, but the scars have shaped who we are today and will be with us for the rest of our lives. Seeing others suffer similar senseless losses opens our wounds anew, and we wonder just how much longer the world can go on like this. Surely the end must be near.

Some claim that tragedy happens only to those strong enough to handle it. But that's just not so. The truth is, we *get* strong because it *did* happen, and most of us have had to search long and hard to find that strength. We are truly a community of wounded soldiers, and somehow just knowing there are others out there who understand helps to ease our pain. For in our darkest hour it's comforting to know we're not alone.

The whole subject of dealing with death is something we don't often want to talk about, as if discussing such a morbid thought might itself bring on tragedy and force us to confront the grief process that we might actually get ready for in advance.

So we do not prepare at all. We walk in blind confidence, praying that death will not touch our household, until one day we find ourselves plunged headlong in the throes of grief and realize we have no idea how to travel this road, how to climb out of this vast crevice that life has unfairly plunged us into. No other experience in life prepares us for such a moment.

Now we are desperate to find someone who will listen to our pain—a pain we are sure is far greater than anyone on earth has ever experienced. We need help. We need guidance. We need to talk to someone who has also traveled this same road, who can weep with us, share our anger and our fears.

I have traveled this road and have come to know the valleys, the hills, and the rocks that stand in the way of healing. It is a journey that I would prefer never to travel again, but I'm sure I will before my life is over. For in loving, we risk the possibility of losing someone we love.

Though my heart cries deepest for the survivors of tragedy, I do hope that others who have not yet experienced a personal loss will take the time to read this book, if for no other reason than to provide meaningful comfort to others who grieve. Many years later we will remember you as the one who was there when we needed a shoulder to cry on. Out of the multitude of stupid things said in comfort and the meaningless catchall offers to help, your words and deeds will stand out as the light in our path through the darkness of despair. You have no idea how much we need you until you experience that need yourself.

To those of you who are presently grieving, I promise that there does exist a way out of this place called The Very Depths of Despair. Once you have passed through it you will never look at the world quite the same. But you can learn to laugh again in between the tears, and you can find hope for tomorrow. So hang on tight and follow me.

THREE

The Downhill Slide

As I watched the towers of the World Trade Center engulfed in flames, its once-strong frame giving way to the ever-increasing burden of concrete above and finally collapsing in a heap of twisted wreckage, I thought of what a fitting picture it painted of the incredible blow death delivers to our hearts. The job of rebuilding it seems almost overwhelming at first. But just as President Bush has promised that New York City will rebuild, in time so shall we.

Nobody expects it to happen overnight. The clean-up alone will take far longer than any of us could have ever imagined. Just getting back on firm ground so we can lay a new foundation is so far ahead of us that we can't begin to envision it yet.

If the physical rebuilding of concrete and steel is such a monumental task, how much greater is the emotional rebuilding of the human heart? Grief is the deepest wound that the human heart must endure. And yet so many of us have unrealistic expectations that the grieving should be able to "snap out of it" and get on with their lives. It simply can't happen that quickly.

Just as rebuilding the city will have to go through stages, so this process called grief has its own steps. Although some of them will feel far from it when we're going through them, all of them are perfectly normal and necessary to our recovery. No set boundaries separate one from another. In fact, several stages may overlap, making them more difficult to bear. It wasn't until I began to research this subject of grief recovery to help others that I realized I went through every one of the stages myself, several of them quite severely.

SHOCK

It comes as no surprise that shock is the first stage. When we first learn that someone we love has died our immediate reaction is disbelief. The mind receives the fatal words, but it cannot comprehend their meaning. By instinct we want to turn back the clock just a few hours to somehow make it all happen differently. After all, the person was fine just a short time ago—happy, healthy, alive! Our minds simply can't accept sudden death or its finality.

Shock allows us to recognize a small piece of the truth at a time by delaying the realization of death until we are more physically and emotionally capable of taking the full blow. Without shock, many of us would literally die from a broken heart.

Symptoms of shock include a racing heart, dizziness or faintness, stomach trouble, loss of appetite, restlessness, or insomnia.

How long does it last? George remained in shock

for four months after the deaths of our children, and we didn't even know it! Since he was handling the loss rather quietly, no one seemed overly concerned about his behavior. They all thought he was coping quite stoically. One day in January he called me from work and said, "Honey, I just came out of shock." It was like driving out of fog into painfully blinding sunlight.

The grief hit him hard after that. He called me from work several times a night, needing to talk and cry, to sort out the emotions that now overwhelmed him. We grieved differently and were not always at the same stage at the same time. But we respected what each needed for healing. Our ability to communicate was the saving grace in our marriage. Without it we probably would have ended up divorced, as do more than half of the couples who lose a child. But we held on when everybody else quit on us, and we got through it together.

DENIAL

Even in the midst of shock there is still denial. This is not happening! We just want to scream No! This precious person that I love did not deserve to die. Here we begin to bargain with God to change what happened. We will do anything to bring our loved one back.

Dreams often invade our sleep—what sleep we do get. We may dream that the loved one isn't dead at all. They're still alive out there somewhere. It's all a hoax, and it's up to us to go find them and bring them home. Then we wake to find them still gone, and the confusion can take several minutes to clear.

Constantly we rewind and replay the tragedy in our minds, trying to make sense of it but still denying it really happened.

ANGER

It doesn't usually take long to get to this stage. Reality begins to sink in and we don't like it! We feel robbed. Victimized. Unjustly shot by the pain in our heart that feels worse than a bullet wound. We may try to inflict pain on others to compensate for it, even if they're not to blame. Or we may verbally or physically attack whoever is convenient.

I grabbed a police officer by the collar and shook him because he revealed to reporters details of my children's deaths before he even told me. I grew up with police officers. My father, my uncle, all their friends—even my husband was once a police officer. I respected the law.

But that night I had no respect for them. The police were there to try to find the killers. They were on my side. But because I could not lash out at the as-yet-unknown murderers, I struck out at the most convenient target. Their presence frustrated me, unsettled my happy, serene lifestyle, kept me from going into my own house, where I was sure my children were still alive. Since they didn't know my children, perhaps my kids had gone for a walk and while they were absent somebody else's kids came in and got shot.

Didn't I tell you that the stages could run together?

George is a peacekeeper by nature, and he was stuck in shock for so long that when the anger did finally catch up with him, his immediate support system had moved on in their lives. So he kept his anger bottled up inside himself. There it stayed to eat away at him for months to come. Finally he went alone to talk to a clergyman. Though he felt somewhat relieved by the visit, I could tell his deepest anger still remained.

Although Stephanie's cancer death seemed a merciful end to her suffering, the same anger arose when she died. I was angry at the silent faceless killer that stalked the darkest recesses of our innocent child's body. I was angry at God for her pain. Angry that all this was happening to my innocent children. Angry because I was left on earth to endure life without them.

Too often people tell us to suppress our anger. But anger itself isn't bad. Even a devout Christian may feel anger and confusion, failing to understand why God allowed something to happen. Friends who comfort us by saying that "It was God's will" only add to our confusion. Anger is a God-given emotion. As humans, we are guided by our sense of right and wrong. We seek what is right in our lives. When something enormously wrong happens, it violates our sense of rightfulness, and we feel angry.

We—or well-meaning people around us—sometimes interpret our anger as an unhealthy sign and try to numb it with drugs or alcohol. In doing so, we only delay the healing. We set ourselves up for long-term addiction that we still must deal with after the initial grief has healed.

Family members took me directly from the police station to a clinic at which I received a tranquilizer that I did not want and insisted I did not need. But those around me thought I was overreacting to my

THE DOWNHILL SLIDE

children's murders. I needed answers about my children's deaths and was quite volatile about it. But they wanted me quiet and out of the way.

The best way to relieve the anger is to admit that it's there and let it happen. Take it out on a wall or other inanimate object. Go off alone and scream out the injustice. After all, it wasn't fair! It didn't have to happen this way! Accept the anger as part of the normal healing process. Then put it behind you and move on.

Sometimes along with anger comes sheer panic. I'm alone! What do I do now? What do I do with all her belongings? What about the funeral? the finances? Where do I start? All these details come crashing down on us at our weakest moment. So we panic. We enter uncharted territory, finding ourselves forced to do things that we've never had to do before. What if we can't meet the challenge—and who asked for it, anyway?

If we are to move on, we must experience the pain of the loss. Anger is a sign that we are getting past the shock and denial and into reality. We are moving forward—and that is good. The more we allow ourselves to experience the pain, the sooner we will begin to adjust.

Researchers conducted a study following an Alaskan earthquake to determine the mental affect it had on its victims. The study determined that those who stayed and faced reminders of the disaster, as well as the continuing aftershocks, adapted more quickly than those who fled the scene or had caring friends "protect" them from the trauma. Those who left the state remained emotionally disturbed and suffered more relationship problems and divorce even years after the tragedy than those who remained and were willing to experience the pain.

It's not healthy for us to run away from the pain. Instead we need to confront it, face up to it. Be an active part of the decisions, the funeral plans, the cleanup—even when it hurts. Don't let others take that away from you by making plans against your wishes. An awareness of this in healing has given me cause for great concern about all the relatives of the missing and confirmed dead who live too far away to meet the physical reality of their grief head-on. Many will find themselves stuck in denial far beyond normal because they were not there to experience in New York or Washington, D.C., the full impact of their loss.

The scenes that play again and again on our television screens allow of us to absorb the reality that distance denies us. Some may consider it a media ploy to gain ratings and play on our emotions. But we all need the repetition to accept the pain of the loss and move on in our grieving. And not one human heart in America has escaped being scarred by this tragedy.

GUILT

As the anger rages through our bodies, guilt takes its allotted place beside it. That's when the "if only's" hit us. If only he hadn't gone to work that day. If only I'd been there to save her. If only he'd been on a lower floor he'd still be alive today. This is guilt, and it feels real. But it's false guilt—unjustified guilt. And it's all part of the grieving. We've got to get to the root of that guilt and then root it out.

Guilt for not doing enough is normal. But we need to analyze that guilt and decide if it is truly justified. If it is, then we must come to terms with it, ask God to forgive us for our actions or failures, and know that we are free from guilt. As human beings we make mistakes. And sometimes the results are forever. We can't turn back the clock no matter how much we loved our lost ones. All we can do is learn from our mistakes so they won't happen again.

Also, we must try to keep our guilt in perspective. Most people don't understand that talking about what happened, going over the details of the loss, trying out different scenarios, is the most effective way we have of resolving our guilt in our own minds.

Rarely do we stop at personal guilt. We find ourselves, justly or not, blaming others, something especially devastating if we place that blame on a family member. The burden of blame begins to chip away not only at him or her, but other family members as well. It can be the most damaging stage of recovery, and the results could be irreparable.

But our humanness, our sense of cause and effect, drives us to blame it on something! We simply cannot cope with the idea that some things just happen—we need an explanation, a reason for it to have occurred. There is always a cause of death on the death certificate, but that's rarely enough. Blame is just another way the heart tries to make sense of the senseless, because we're still fighting this whole reality issue with every fiber of our being.

If we can actually pin the blame on a perpetrator,

we have a target for our vengeance. And we can devise all manner of justifiable punishments to soothe our suddenly barren souls. The whole blame issue is a volatile one, and you'll get plenty of unasked-for advice from well-meaning friends and clergy as you seek to make sense of the crime. The men who hijacked those planes were murderers of the basest kind. We have every right to want justice in the face of such horrific loss. But because this chapter deals only with the downhill stages of grief, we'll briefly address the vengeance debate in another chapter.

DEPRESSION AND LONELINESS

The grieving process is a roller-coaster of emotions changing not just daily but sometimes hourly. The anger can make us feel strong and powerful, capable of ripping someone apart with our bare hands. On the other hand, the guilt and loneliness leave us feeling weak, drained of all physical ability.

During the time all these stages are ravaging our emotions we still have to make so many decisions, so many adjustments to everyday life, and deal with so many variables in the individuals affected by the loss, that it's a wonder we come out of it at all.

Teetering between denial and reality, we often seek to retrieve or locate the dead person. As we may call out to them we fully expect a response. Preoccupied with thoughts of the loved one or reliving painful memories, we long for them to return. Then, as we begin to accept the fact that the dead are not coming back, the loneliness hits hardest. It leaves us confused, afraid, and in deep despair. And the support system we clung to in the early stages of grief has already given up and expects us to be getting on with our lives. Friends and relatives don't want to talk about it anymore—just at the time when we need it most.

Everyone around us has returned to their daily routine, leaving us to wonder how they can do that after what happened. Often we just want to bail out, shut ourselves away from society, because no one understands the pain we continue to feel. The world seems suddenly strange and cold—and it may not be just our imagination. Most of us really don't know how to handle a grieving person. Too often our friends simply avoid us because they don't know what to say.

The friends who do try to comfort us say all the wrong things. The advice they offer may be very good, but they present it too soon. As a result we may become defensive of our emotions, even amplifying them to display to our friends that what we are feeling is real.

Although our friends may tell us not to dwell on our loss, we may spend hours in a daze, unaware of the world around us while we lose ourselves in the past—that wonderful past when our loved one was alive! We find ourselves dwelling on the intimate details of that unique individual's life, freezing his or her face in time so we will never forget it.

The house goes to the dogs, and for some reason we just don't care. Even the simplest chores are burdensome. We sigh a lot and experience an enormous sense of worthlessness and idleness. Our intense longing to hear the familiar voice makes the silence almost deafening.

After my children died I felt as if encased in a cold hollow 55-gallon drum. I screamed for help—for answers to explain why this was happening to my family—but my words just echoed back at me. There appeared no way out of the drum, and nobody seemed interested in rescuing me.

A neighbor of mine, who also experienced a tragic event in her life, told me that she felt as if she had fallen into a deep well. She too said it was dark and cold, with no escape.

All these sensations suggest a feeling of being imprisoned in a situation over which you have no control. You are an innocent victim being unjustly punished. And nobody seems to care.

What we don't realize is that many do care very much. They just don't know how to show it. It's easy for people to jump on the bandwagon of flag waving and candle lighting, and memorial services for the victims as a whole. But when it comes to comforting the survivors one at a time, most of them are at a total loss for what to say. Their discomfort may leave you feeling like an alien in your own town. You want to cut yourself away from the rest of the world. "Stop the world and let me off!" you cry. If only you could go back to where your loved one stopped and then stay there forever.

This deep state of depression is the time when we need to force ourselves to hold to a regular routine of waking and eating. Set the alarm to give your day order. It's too easy to fall into the trap of despair if we never get dressed, sleep till noon, and stay up to watch old movies till the early morning hours.

We must also make an effort to get back out into the world. A new outfit, a new hairdo, lunch with a friend can all give us that little lift we need to help us over the rough spots. If nobody will invite you to lunch, then call and invite them. It's not being extravagant or disloyal to the deceased. It can, however, be very helpful in getting you over this hump.

It is here where the upward side of grieving begins. Having reached the bottom of the hill and now traveling in the lowest regions of the valley of despair, it's time to start looking up toward recovery.

FOUR

Why Don't They Grieve Like Me?

That's all she ever talked about," Paul complained about his now ex-wife. "Ryan's death was hard for both of us. But I needed to put Ryan's things out of sight and pick up the pieces. Patty turned the whole house into a shrine!

"I just kept coming home later and later, unable to face the reminders of my son's death. After a while I began to feel as if maybe I didn't love him as much as she did, because I just wanted it to be over—and she said it would never be. God, how I loved my son! But I can't bring him back, and it rips me apart."

The fact that we all grieve differently can sometimes tear us away from the people we love most. We know what we need for our own healing, so why doesn't she require the same thing?

The grieving process usually takes between six months and three years. That doesn't mean it's all over after that, but it does suggest that by then we've pretty well filled in the crater left by the bomb dropped on us, tamped it down, and are standing fairly firm again. We've also mapped out a new routine that meets our daily needs.

But many factors determine how long we grieve and even *how* we grieve. They include: The age of the deceased and the cause of death. Whether or not we had time to prepare for the death. Our relationship with the one who has deceased. Our own age, gender, and personality. Our individual coping ability. Our cultural, ethnic, and religious beliefs. Our experiences with previous losses. And the strength of our support system.

Let's spend some time looking at some of these variables to see why we as individuals grieve the way we do and why we even grieve differently from loss to loss.

CAUSE OF DEATH

The cause of death is the first thing that begins to color how we will grieve. We all hope to live long fruitful lives and die quietly in our sleep at a ripe old age. When an older family member dies of natural causes we accept it as part of the life cycle, though we still feel we've been robbed of someone important to us.

Sadly, there seem to be far more wrongful deaths than rightful ones. The wrongful deaths produce much more trauma for us. Deaths of children or young adults are almost always considered wrongful deaths, because young people are not supposed to die. The anger at the injustice of losing someone wrongfully can be intense. Wrongful death tends to leave us feeling more vulnerable, more mortal, and rocks our faith in a Supreme Being more severely.

Whether or not we have had time to prepare ourselves for the death also determines how we grieve. An expected death, such as that following a terminal illness, gives us a forewarning and a chance to prepare emotionally for the loss. If we accept the inevitable, we even have time to get ourselves right with the dying person. We have opportunity to think about all the things that will need to be done. So our transition into the loss is not so abrupt.

Sudden death, however, permits no emotional preparation. Here we are going about a normal day and *Boom!* The bomb drops right on our hearts before we can even get our guard up. We don't get a chance to say goodbye or I'm sorry or I love you. September 11, 2001, violently and unexpectedly left America numb. Such loss is far more disruptive to our lives. The details that we must take care of *now!* threaten to overwhelm us.

A violent death can trigger just as violent grief. We experience considerable guilt, and not just anger, but rage! The details of what happened traumatize us. What could we have done to stop it? Did they suffer? Did they cry out for us? And we need a reason to explain why it happened at all. If we can just pinpoint a cause, we can predict and prevent future losses. It's easier to dodge the bullets if we know which direction they're coming from.

George and I still suffer with that even today. It's no longer grief, but a whole lifestyle of bullet ducking, something we'll never overcome. Somebody must always be on guard for the family so it won't happen again.

RELATIONSHIP

Our relationship with the one who has died, and how satisfied we were with that relationship, also determines how we grieve. As a child I lost both an 8-year-old cousin and a teenage friend to leukemia. Naturally, I was closer to my cousin. Losing her was also my first encounter with death, a fact that would play a part in shaping my reaction to further deaths in my life. But my grief would have been more severe if that loss had been a parent or a sibling.

As adults, most of us expect to one day bury our parents. But only after they die do we realize the extent of what we've lost. No matter how old we are, we suddenly feel like an orphan. Losing a parent as a child is far more traumatic. There goes a child's security right out the window! In chapter 6 we'll talk more about kids and grief and how we can be effective in comforting them.

Losing a spouse is especially difficult. Everything that was "ours" is now just "mine." "We" is now just "I." Like having a part of yourself cut away, it takes time to start thinking as an individual again, and the thought of it seems almost incomprehensible. We feel tremendous guilt over thoughts of being disloyal to the dead spouse, and raising the kids alone seems almost impossible at first.

Losing a child is considered the most devastating kind of loss. Parents too often find themselves torn apart because they may blame themselves or each other for not protecting the child. And since they are each grieving in their own way, they can't offer the moral support the other needs. The divorce rate within a year of losing a child is more than 70 percent. Why? Because parents can't comfort each other. They can't understand their different needs. It adds tragedy to tragedy and just doesn't have to be.

PERSONALITY

Everybody's personality is unique. Many of you may be familiar with a personality test that determines if you are melancholy, sanguine, choleric, phlegmatic, or a combination of them. The test I took revealed that I am a choleric melancholy. My husband is a phlegmatic melancholy. Knowing this helped me to understand why we grieved differently when confronted with the same loss. Find yourself among the four types.

Melancholy: Melancholies live by emotions. Easily hurt by other people's callousness, they tend to suffer most from sadness and depression after loss. They relive every detail of the past, unable to let go of either good memories or horrible ones.

I wore a bracelet engraved with the names of all five children for the first full year to keep them close to me. That was the melancholy coming out in me. George and I both welcomed a conversation about the kids anytime, so we were able to share this aspect of our grieving together.

Choleric: Cholerics are the ones who get things done among us. They do not stop until they have finished the task and will step over anything that gets in the way. At the World Trade Center they were the ones who grabbed the buckets and began the task of sifting through the rubble. Strong-willed, they refuse to give up until they have all their questions answered. Prone to drive themselves to exhaustion, they can easily be pushed to unreasonable anger, becoming irate and hot-tempered.

Boy, that was me! And there were certain things I had to do to satisfy that anger that George did not understand. Everybody who tried to shield me from the loss was doing the exact opposite of what my choleric personality was telling me I needed for my healing.

Phlegmatic: Phlegmatics are the steady workers with a slow, even temperament. Nothing can rush them. When sudden death catches phlegmatics off guard, forcing them to make quick decisions that go against their personality, their systems simply shut down. That's why George remained in shock for four months. The loss just ran over him like a runaway train, because he could not quicken his pace to match it.

Phlegmatics need to slow things down so that the grief process matches their steady progression of things. That was hard for an angry take-charge choleric like me to understand. George couldn't possibly match my pace as I charged ahead in search of answers to my grieving.

Sanguine: Sanguines are the cheerful socialites among us. For them, life is a party to enjoy. Although the first to volunteer, they rarely finish what they start. In loss they tend to be more optimistic that it'll all work out somehow. When confronted with horrific tragedy, they simply cannot fathom the horror on their television screens and may need to turn away to balance their naturally happy lives. They just want to get past all this—to put it behind them and move forward.

So what happens when you have a choleric married to a sanguine? The choleric needs to confront his grief by talking it out and finding the facts. The sanguine wants to put it behind her and move on, especially since thinking about it is just too painful for such a naturally happy person to deal with. We need to ask ourselves, What kinds of conflicts will this cause? Can they communicate? Can they share their grief easily? What can they do to prevent a breakup in their marriage? Above all, we must remember that each must be free to seek outside help to do what each needs for his or her own healing.

When we choose a life mate, we tend to gravitate toward someone who will balance our own personality. The union works because of that balance. I like to tell people that I make George get out of his chair and get something done, and he forces me to sit down and take a break before I kill myself. We're both better people because we have each other.

Grief throws us into the extremes of our personalities, knocking our ship off-kilter and threatening to sink us entirely as we struggle to fight the waves hitting us broadside. We will discuss this more fully in the next chapter. If you and your spouse find yourselves in conflict over your grieving, what we discuss there might just save your marriage.

MEN VERSUS WOMEN

Not only our personality but our gender affects how we grieve. Societal attitudes about the genders also play a part.

Western culture teaches men to buck up, be

strong, handle it like a man. Women can faint and fall apart and turn to Jell-O. American society considers them the genteel sex, unable to handle things the way men can. And yet research has proved that women can handle physical pain better than men.

Females usually have no trouble seeking out a friend to talk to—a crutch to prop them up so they don't fall. Once they find that crutch they will cling to it throughout the ordeal. But a man usually won't reach out for something to steady himself. He tries to stand against the winds of adversity and endure it "like a man" even if a tree that could support him is right beside him.

AGE

Our age also plays a part in how we grieve. Older people begin to accept death as part of life. It's tragic, we know, but it happens, and we can't do anything about it. At the same time, the instance of a surviving spouse dying within a year of the death of a mate is alarmingly high. The age-weakened body can't bounce back from the physical strain of loss. And since older mourners accept death more easily, it is easier for them to give up their will to carry on alone.

Teens probably have the hardest time dealing with loss. The teenage years are such a difficult period for any emotion. Daring bravado and invincibility mix with vulnerability and horrendous fear of ridicule. Death is a difficult issue for such semi-independent minds to comprehend. What they don't understand they either clam up about because they're too old to ask, or they react physically or violently to the loss.

Children between the ages of 5 and 12 also have a tough time. They respond more keenly to the injustice of loss because they don't understand why somebody they love had to die. Living in a world where authority is out of their hands, they are wholly dependent on adults and feel helpless to change what has happened in their lives. Next to teens, they take death hardest.

RELIGIOUS OR CULTURAL BELIEFS

Whether we have great hope or no hope beyond this life affects the degree of our grieving. What do we believe about the hereafter? Who gets to go? Is this a permanent or a temporary loss? Are our loved ones asleep or can they see us? Are they in a good place or a bad place or somewhere in between? Will we be together again someday?

I had little hope when the doctors diagnosed Steph with cancer, but that hope blossomed when I started reading about God's plan of salvation. God was in control, and His plan made all the sense in the world. It was a tremendous comfort to me. We'll be talking more in depth in a later chapter.

COPING RANGE

How we accept the pain of loss will determine whether we rise above it or succumb to it. Our will to be bigger than the pain is vital to healthy recovery. Those who feel helpless and have no great desire to live are more apt to succumb to the situation and die.

The Holocaust is a perfect example. Those who walked out of the German concentration camps found themselves compelled to survive at all costs. One of their main driving forces was to live to tell the world of the atrocities they had endured—to defeat the Nazis simply by refusing to die. For many who endured, just knowing there was one person outside the camp walls who cared that they lived at all meant the difference between hopelessness and hope. Faith that God is with us in all circumstances can give us the mental fortitude to stand up to any situation.

The survivors of the Holocaust became politicians, doctors, and lawyers—strong men and women with wills of iron and tremendous coping ranges. In chapter 12 we'll talk about how we too can widen our coping range so that we might withstand even the fiercest storms.

Now that you better understand why you grieve the way you do, go back and try to see the same loss from the perspective of other family members. In the next chapter we'll discuss how we can use this new understanding to strengthen our ties to loved ones we still hold dear.

FIVE

Family Ties

Needless to say, with all these variables, grief can have a profound effect on our families and our marriages, especially when two people in the same family grieve very differently and are too stubborn to allow the other the space he or she needs to heal. Loyalties appear to get trampled when one seeks outside help that the other feels is unnecessary, or when one takes up the brunt of the physical burden now that another has died.

If we are to save our families, each member must learn to work it out together. Sometimes that means allowing each other the freedom and encouragement to do whatever is necessary to the individual's healing. The keys to any good relationship are unity, communication, and respect.

We all need to know that we're not alone in our loss, and believe me, with all the grief in this world, we're never alone. If we don't already know somebody who can share our grief, we can find them in other places, such as a community grief recovery group.

Many feel reluctant to join such a group. But

those who do find a family of wounded soldiers who can sympathize—who will never tell us to quit talking about it, snap out of it, and get on with our lives. Meeting individuals several years down the road to recovery can give us an idea of what we can expect in our own healing.

Often couples choose divorce after a loss, a second loss heaped onto the first one. Although the statistics are tragic, many marriages and families could have remained intact if only they could have learned to respect the needs of each family member. Our first priority is to keep the lines of communication open. If they are already closed, get them reopened, even if it takes a mediator to do it. Not only is there no disgrace in asking for help, but there *is* honor in trying to save what you have.

Ask a minister or a counselor to act as your go-between. But make sure you find one experienced in the grief process, or you may wind up with just one more person in the circle at a loss for what to do. Sometimes your own pastor may not be your best choice. Your local hospital may help you contact a hospice volunteer who has experience dealing with the grief-stricken. With or without a mediator, each family member needs a chance to talk it out and tell how the loss is affecting him or her. What are his fears, what does he miss most, and how has this loss changed his life forever? What does she need to do to say goodbye, to honor the loved one and move on in the grief process? For each member the answers will differ. But even the youngest members of the family have needs that must be met if they are to find their way through the valley of grief. Those children who do not get the support they must have in their younger years will suffer scars that will affect their grieving later in life.

During tragedy we must assure children that we will not abandon them, that they will continue to be cared for. As we observed earlier, children live in a world in which they have little authority or control, and precious little life experience. Thus they need security and nurturing. We cannot expect them to become the man or woman of the house after a parent dies. Junior is no substitute father, and Missy can't meet all the daily demands that motherhood entails. The remaining parent is still wholly responsible for the child. A new spirit of family unity and cooperation to meet new responsibilities must evolve. But the child's activities, interests, and friends should remain active.

Husbands need to be able to lean on their wives, and their spouses may have to invite them to do so by asking some questions that will draw them out and allow them to let out the emotions males tend to bottle up inside. Men must be assured that if they let the dam break and spill, their wives will keep it in confidence.

Wives need to understand that men do not grieve the same way they do. Males seem to feel that they must remain strong for the family's sake even though inside they may be collapsing. Some men assume that they must hug and comfort everyone else, when in actuality they would rather crawl up onto someone's lap and cry like a baby. Be there for your husband. Let him know that he can express his feelings freely without fear of ridicule or betrayal. If he feels like crying, let him do it.

Generally wives find it easier to open up to their husbands and expect to be able to lean on them. They accomplish it with varying degrees of success, unless the husband has so bottled up his emotions to keep from breaking down that he won't converse at all. Even under the best circumstances, women tend to talk 40 percent more than men, and most men don't want to stick around long enough to hear all that a woman needs to say. This is where lunch with a friend can help a woman fulfill that extra wordage necessary for her to find healing, without exhausting her mate.

A man may need to say it in fewer words, but he too can find great comfort in spending time with a male friend to work out the male side of grief. Since few men are "go to lunch" types, a fishing or sports outing may be just what he needs, especially since it may take him longer than a woman to open up to a friend.

A trip of several days gives him a chance to warm up to the idea of opening up and relieving all that loss entails. Though it may be difficult for his wife to get through those same days at home without him, it may be the best gift she can give her mate. When he returns she'll see the difference in his face. And with this weight lifted from him even a little bit, the husband and wife can move forward together.

Not only should we honor the different needs of the individual, we must respect those things that may be painful to another. If you need to look at photo albums or view the body or keep some special mementos and your spouse longs to put it behind them, both of those needs can be met individually without stepping over the boundaries of the other. And it must be done for proper healing of both. But most of all, don't let such things draw you apart.

Grief is a time of upside-down, topsy-turvy emotions—feeling one way one minute and another the next. Remembering a happy day in the morning and crying your eyes out in the afternoon. It is often a time of laughing and crying, loving and hating, feeling strong and feeling weak, remembering the richness of the past and at the same time hurting for what now can never be. There exists no one "right way" to feel after the death of a loved one. All these emotions are perfectly normal and play a part in the healing process.

The fact that emotions will attack each family member at different times of the day and week will strain the family unit. To compensate, find something that you can all agree on or benefit from and do it. Buy something the family will enjoy, take a trip, or plan an outing that all will appreciate.

A time of bereavement is a good time to splurge a little. Just a few days after Stephanie died, George and I bought a new camera with an extra 200-millimeter lens to take on a trip to western Kansas, where George had bird hunted for years. We took lots of pictures en route and enjoyed being alone together away from the reminders of the tragedy that had befallen us and the scores of well-meaning friends and family trying to lighten our load with unasked-for advice. It was a good healing time for us. An outdoor camera was something we had wanted for a long time.

But we would not have bought it if a friend had not given us permission to do something foolish.

Hundreds of people had donated to memorial funds to help us cover the funeral costs of burying five children. Then, as he handed George a check, a friend said, "Spend it on yourselves. Go get something you've been wanting for a long time." Financially, it was not a responsible thing to do. Recovery-wise, it was excellent.

I am giving you that permission now. Even something as small as a new board game can help bring a few smiles back into the family circle. A day trip to the next town, with its new surroundings and less-familiar activities, can give you the space you need to breathe in deep, fill your lungs, and try to catch up to your emotions. Sometimes when we can stand back and look at our troubles from a distance, we can gain a better perspective on where we need to go from here. There is no dishonor in this, and it's not really running away. It's absorbing the enormity of the loss in pieces that are small enough to cope with. Reality still hurts too much to live it every moment right now.

Many grieving people feel guilty about taking such a trip immediately following a death, and even more guilty if they find themselves enjoying it. But you may actually find it therapeutic. It is not shameful to have good times during mourning. We need those moments to give us ballast against the storm, to prevent us from tipping sideways into a deep depression that can take a long time to set right again.

Unity. Communication. Respect. That's what we must strive for to keep our family unit healthy. Love builds a strong ship, but it is the ballast that we need most to keep us upright in the midst of life's storms.

It takes more than the pilot at the wheel to maintain the ship on course, and strong knots to hold the sails on their masts.

Family ties are the strongest bonds on earth. God gave us families that we might more fully understand the love that our heavenly Father feels toward us. Nothing hurts worse than losing someone we love. But in losing, we can better realize the incredible sacrifice that God willingly made when He gave His Son to die for us.

And in losing, we also come to realize how important we are to each other. Death makes us appreciate just how precious life is and how much we need our loved ones in our lives. We can use the loss in a positive way to strengthen our ties, set our sails, and pack in the ballast to keep our ship upright. If we let go of each other, we allow the ship to sink.

Make a copy of the Family Pact at the end of this chapter and display it where it can remind the whole family that none of us is going through this alone. Use it as a tool to pack in the ballast your own family ship needs to stay upright in these troubled waters.

OUR FAMILY PACT

WHILE WE ARE GRIEVING:

1. Privacy will be respected. We all need time to be alone.

2. Hugs are available upon request to any family member who requires one.

3. Crying is not only allowed, it is encouraged, for it is a healthy part of grieving.

4. From time to time we'll talk about our loss to make sure we're each doing OK.

5. We know that holidays will be harder now, and we'll be there for each other to get through them.

6. We'll all try to be tolerant of irritations that we are all bound to feel, recognizing that this too will pass as time goes by.

7. We will allow each family member the full time they must have to heal.

8. We respect the fact that sometimes someone outside of the family can be the most effective help for us.

9. We also recognize that the world will forget our tragedy long before we have healed, and we must stick together to the finish.

10. We'll all have our weak moments. No one person will be expected to always be strong for the rest.

11. We'll try hard to take everyone's feelings into account when making decisions about what to dispose of and what to keep.

12. We will not be judgmental over any temporary loss of faith. It is part of our grieving. The answers to our questions will come with time. God is patient with His children. We must be too.

Six

Kids Grieve Too

Seven-year-old Kevin was filled with guilt over his father's death. He knew it was all his fault, knew that was why everybody kept sending him off to play. The next-door neighbor had watched him while all the people who loved Daddy went to the funeral. Only Kevin didn't get to say goodbye.

He hated himself. And he hated the squirt gun he just had to have, the last thing his father bought for him because he had cried until Daddy gave in. Now Daddy was dead. Kevin knew it was his fault. If he hadn't squirted the front tires of Daddy's car, it would have stopped and Daddy would be alive. The boy buried his face in his arms and cried.

Loss affects children far more than most of us realize. A lot of the things we do to protect them from grieving only isolates them in their grief and forces them to deal with it alone. Most adults don't realize that children grieve just as hard or harder than we do. They experience guilt just as we do, and they need to work out the details of what happened to help them to dispel that guilt.

Kevin wasn't responsible for his father's death. A little water squirted on the tires didn't cause the brakes to fail. But to a 7-year-old boy that seems very logical. Doesn't he deserve real answers to dispel his very real guilt, so that he can get on with the next stage of grieving? We mustn't pooh-pooh what sound to us like ridiculous ideas. Children need answers. If we ignore their questions, they will find answers for them somehow, and sometimes those explanations are far worse than reality. A child can get stuck in denial, especially if we keep them away from the funeral and other arrangements or farm them out to friends until it all blows over. Not getting to say goodbye can stunt their progress in working through their grief.

Children over the age of 4 who want to attend the funeral should be allowed to do so. Curious children will pay attention and seek those things necessary to their healing. Nothing they will see or hear will be worse than what their mind is already telling them. There will be times during and after the service when children don't act as if they are grieving at all. A child will run down the hall, or wander away to pick flowers on other people's graves. But that's the young mind's way of dealing with the sadness. An immature emotional system can't handle too much sadness all at once. So it does it in little bits, taking breaks as need be until the young person can handle a little more.

Allow the child to feel involved by giving him a flower or letting her pick some from the garden to give to the person who has died, whether that involves placing it on the person's chest in an open casket ceremony, or on the casket itself. This encourages the children to say goodbye and face the reality of the loss. It also makes them feel that their love was as important as that of the adults who can afford to buy whole bouquets of flowers.

Nightmares are tied to denial, or to the death itself. They are a young mind's way of dealing with its perception of what has happened. Children may show hostility toward the deceased for letting them down. Or they may consider the loved one a saint, and as a result nobody will ever be able to fill the person's shoes.

People tell them Grandpa's in heaven, which is a happy place, but they're all crying as they say it. It confuses a child. We must be careful to call death what it is. People are dead; they have died. They have not gone on a trip, or passed on, or gone to sleep, or been "lost." Children don't understand these words beyond their literal meanings, and cannot begin to adjust to the permanency of death until they realize that death is irreversible and the loved one cannot come back.

By the age of 5 children can grasp that death is final. They need to have their questions about it answered. If you don't know the answer, tell them you don't know, but that you'll try to find out. And do so! Ask your local hospice or funeral home if they have any material to help children deal with loss. Check out the library for books that deal with grief on a child's level, and read it first to make sure it says what your child needs to hear. Talk to a pastor. Do your best to give accurate information.

Don't answer by saying, "God took him." Such a response can frighten a child; they may think, *He may take me next!* God didn't cause the death. It was cancer, a heart attack, a car accident, a horrible crime. Explain the real cause of death on the child's level. Don't try to cover it up, candy-coat it, or keep secrets. Death is not a happy event, but a harsh reality that must be faced, and the sooner children understand that, the easier they will find it to get on with their life. Help them to understand that it won't always hurt as bad as it does at the moment. But don't try to rush them through the grief stages.

Dads, don't be afraid to show how you feel. A son may conclude that because his father doesn't cry, he mustn't either. As a human being you feel pain at the loss of someone you love. Don't stifle these feelings. Tears are a safety valve. They allow you to release the pressure before it reaches the explosion point. Let us not forget that even Jesus wept, and He was the manliest person our world ever knew.

Anger is as real to children as it is to adults. If we do not help them properly channel such feelings, it can lead to bigger problems later on. A child may need counseling from you or from someone else who can direct their anger in an acceptable way. Make sure the child's teachers are aware of the situation so they can be available to talk or to permit the child to step out of the room as needed. Emotions rush in at odd times, and I don't think there's a child out there who wants to cry in front of the whole class.

Following a loss, a child's grades will usually fall for the rest of that school year. Let me give you an example.

My husband lost his father from a heart attack when he was in the eighth grade. George and his dad were best friends. True outdoor enthusiasts, they enjoyed

hunting and fishing together. The two had been plan-
ning a duck-hunting trip up north in the fall. In fact,
they had spent the last hours of his father's life together
at the shooting range practicing for duck season. A short
time after they returned home, his father died.

The loss overwhelmed George, an only son, and
his questions about death remained unanswered. That
night well-meaning neighbors sent him to the movies
so they could minister to the needs of his mother.
George's grades at school plummeted to D's and F's
and stayed there for the rest of the year.

Recently, while going through a box of photographs and mementos left by his mother, I came
across one of George's old report cards. I was about to
chide him about the terribly low grades and how *he*
was one to talk about our children's grades when I
suddenly realized that what I held in my hand was
proof of the suffering a young boy had experienced
when he lost his father and best friend.

Nothing on George's report card said anything
about the pain he had endured. A stranger looking at
the record could easily conclude that laziness had
caused his failure. George hadn't lollygagged the year
away. He spent it in a cave of grief, unable to crawl
out of it as the world passed him by. Nobody did anything to help him understand his loss or to prepare
him for the losses he would endure later on.

When grades do suffer, especially if they plummet
quite noticeably, ask the teacher to include information about the death in the school records. If it is not
done, the record may follow the child throughout
their school years without any explanation as to the

reason they did poorly that particular year. It could cause undeserved repercussions later on in life, especially if the child is in high school. A few years from now colleges may pass the child by as they look at grades to decide who will get the scholarships.

We can't expect bereaved persons to function at top performance for a while after the death of a loved one no matter how old they are. Make sure the school understands this, and be firm with them if they don't. Pushing and insisting that children buckle down to their studies will only add pressure to their already weakened hearts. But encouragement and understanding will help them to continue to strive.

After a loss a new pet can be great therapy. Unconditional kisses from a little wet tongue, the new responsibility of caring for something alive, can build a child's self-esteem and the incentive to hang in there when it hurts. Give the child a photograph of the loved one to keep in their room, their wallet, or their locket. Encourage them to draw pictures or write stories about how they feel today. It may be necessary for them to write a letter to the loved one, expressing what the loss means to them.

As the pain of the loss fades, talk about the wonderful times you shared with the loved one and remember the special qualities that made the person shine in your life. Teach the child that our memories are things that we can hold on to forever, that not even death can steal them away from us. In this way, we teach our children to look at grief as a healthy, human experience, and that their feelings matter just as much as those of adults.

SEVEN

The Uphill Climb

The process we call grief recovery is much like sledding down a very steep hill. The downhill slide is so fast that it almost takes our breath away, until we reach the bottom and find ourselves alone in the silence. It may take us a while to gather our wits. But at some point we realize that the only way to get back home is to pick up that heavy sled and start the long, arduous climb back up the hill. The slow uphill climb of grief requires the most time and conscious effort to accomplish.

TRYING TO ADJUST

At some point we have to begin to adjust to the fact that the loved one isn't coming back, and now we've got to learn to fill in where the person left off. All those things we did together—the gardening, the taxes, and the other little jobs we once shared—are just memories now. It takes time to start a new life. We'll make some mistakes as we learn new responsibilities and new skills that we never had to deal with before. And that's OK. It's all part of the process of trying to adjust.

After we went from a family of seven to a couple almost overnight, I had a hard time cooking for two. I'd open a bag of frozen corn and pour the whole thing into a pot. Going to bed without the responsibility of checking on the kids was extremely difficult to get used to, so accustomed was I to the chores of parenthood at bedtime.

After loss our whole world is different now. And we're having a tough time adjusting. But we're doing it because we have little choice. As we deal with the silence, we're even learning to adjust to how our friends treat us and how to respond to difficult questions such as "What does your husband do?" or "How many kids do you have?"

I couldn't answer that last one easily for years without including the ones we lost. *Sure, they're dead,* I reasoned. *But they have lived! They're still my children and I will count them as such.* Today when I meet someone casually I can usually tell them about just my three living children. But if I know I'm going to be seeing the person a lot, they have to know what happened so I can talk about all my kids in conversations in the future. This way I maintain the right of every other parent in the room to talk about *all* my children and their antics when they were young.

Relatives may begin pressuring you to make decisions about property that belonged to the loved one. The vultures are circling in search of their cut of the spoils. So it's a good idea to put off making big decisions until you can think straight to avoid mistakes you'll regret later. Wait a while to sell the house or the extra car. Don't let relatives pressure you into giving them things you may not really want to part with, or items that you could sell at market value to help cover all the expenses that accumulated while you were still in shock.

You have plenty of time to decide what to keep and how best to liquidate the other stuff. When you know you're ready, treat the really precious things as if you were donating body organs. Give them to people who will really use them and appreciate them for what they are.

We know adjustment has come when we put the loved one's things away. While we can keep the photos on the mantel or still display a few special trophies or ribbons, we can't keep everything, and we shouldn't make shrines out of rooms.

AFFIRMING REALITY

Losing a loved one is a complex loss of many facets of our own lives. We say goodbye not just to a body but also to the things we did together and for each other. It is a process that takes place in bits and pieces as we encounter them, and as we learn to accept that we'll never do those things again. For example, we may say goodbye to taking the child to school, to fixing him breakfast, to watching her practice her trumpet, or to their being in the school play. With adults we say goodbye to breakfast together in the morning, to goodnight kisses, to making love.

It may take months to confront some of these goodbyes. Every day we encounter more things that we have to say goodbye to, and some are harder than others. The planned things that now will never happen—vacations, next year's garden, retirement together. Adjusting to birthdays, holidays, and anniversaries can be especially difficult.

REINVESTING

Now that the reality has sunk in and we have said the goodbyes, it's time to climb back onto the merry-go-round of life and reinvest our energy into new relationships and new activities. The busy whirl of activities may leave us spinning at first, but we'll soon catch up to the pace of normal life again.

HEALING

This stage can be a long time in coming. Healing means being able to remember without crying. The guilt is behind you. The excruciating pain of the amputation has faded enough to be bearable to live with now. You understand that being happy isn't disloyalty to the loved one, and you no longer feel guilty if you forget to think about the person for a day.

I remember vividly the first day I didn't think about the kids. It was our daughter Sandy's first birthday. Sandy was born 11 months after their deaths. I was so wrapped up in her party with relatives—celebrating our beautiful 1-year-old that God had blessed us with—that I completely forgot about the other kids until 10:00 that night.

Lying in bed, going over the events of the day, I suddenly realized I hadn't thought about them all day long. Tears burned my cheeks like acid. I vowed I'd never forget again. Years later, I still think about the kids on a regular basis. They are a part of who I am and always will be. But I don't make a concentrated effort to focus on them, and I don't go into hysterics if I find that I got so busy that they didn't enter my thoughts during a particular day. I can't say exactly when that change came about or even how long it took to get there. It was a process rather than a moment.

RECOVERY

Recovery occurs slowly and inconsistently, rather than all at once. You may feel better for a while, then much worse. Depending on the relationship of the lost loved one and the age at which the person died, such emotional swings can last several years. You achieve recovery when you can think about the loved one without overwhelming sadness and can invest yourself in other thoughts and activities. As you acknowledge the reality, grief fades into treasured memories. That is the goal of grieving: to treasure the memories and to live a full life enriched by the lives that have touched us.

Study the chart below and decide where you are in the grieving process right now. Don't be surprised if you find yourself between two stages. As long as you don't find yourself stuck in one stage too long, you are experiencing normal grief and can expect the process to continue to run its course.

MY PERSONAL PROGRESS

(WHERE I'M AT RIGHT NOW)

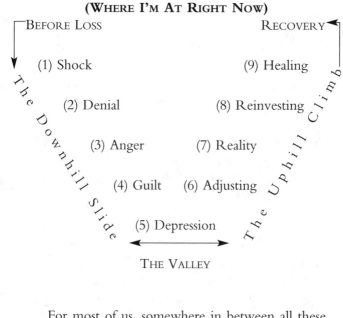

BEFORE LOSS   RECOVERY

(1) Shock   (9) Healing

(2) Denial   (8) Reinvesting

(3) Anger   (7) Reality

(4) Guilt   (6) Adjusting

(5) Depression

The Downhill Slide   *The Uphill Climb*

THE VALLEY

For most of us, somewhere in between all these stages a nagging need for bigger answers beyond the tragedy starts to gnaw its way into the center of our minds. Questions that never mattered all that much now seem vital to our recovery. Like huge rocks in our path, they hinder that long climb upward. I hope the chapters that follow will help you find your way around them.

EIGHT

Search for Strength

Jack was the oldest of three children. By age 19 he had lost his father and had taken on the responsibility of being father to his younger brother and sister. Out of sheer necessity he had learned to be responsible. When the need arose he could be strong and take charge.

When four of his grandchildren were murdered, he was there immediately to offer support to his daughter and son-in-law. He identified the bodies to spare the parents the anguish of the gruesome sight and took care of the finances during the time the parents were unable to think clearly. Then he opened his home to them for two months and provided support until his son-in-law had recovered enough to work at a job once more.

Jack was a veritable port in a storm. But he lost his own job in the midst of this family tragedy because his employer could not deal with the grief the bereaved family had to endure. But through it all, Jack kept his head.

And yet, 10 years later, he admitted, "Having to

be strong for everyone else and keep everything together was the most difficult thing I ever had to do. I
still wish I could just curl up in somebody's lap and
cry. I have never been allowed to do that."

Jack is my father, and without his strength George
and I would have found it much harder to survive our
crisis. Though I admire his ability to have held everything together for us all, as I now look back, I realize
that Dad took the brunt of the burden alone. Even 10
years later he had not found the comfort and strength
that can be gained only by depending wholly on God.
If only he could have known that he has a Father in
heaven, who knows how badly he hurts. Yet it was
through this same tragedy that I came to know this
God of all comfort as I do. His Word promises:

"(For the Lord thy God is a merciful God;) he
will not forsake thee" (Deuteronomy 4:31).

"God is our refuge and strength, a very present
help in trouble" (Psalm 46:1).

It's difficult to be strong amid the turmoil when
tragedy strikes. Sometimes the harder you try, the
more you begin to crumble under the weight. It requires an enormous amount of strength to endure the
death of a loved one.

I have always considered myself to be strong-
willed—rather like my father, I must admit. I certainly wasn't like those women in the movies who
faint at the first hint of adversity. When my children
were killed, my anger provided me with the strength
to withstand my loss that first night. I vowed I would
not lose my head. Ten hours at the police station kept
my anger at fever pitch.

The next day, while I was sitting idly in a dark motel room with orders not to leave town "until notified," my mind had a chance to focus on what had really happened. Sitting there alone made me recognize how quiet and lonely my life was going to be without my children. It was then that I realized I was *not* strong enough to endure this ordeal alone. Clinging to the morning newspaper, I gazed longingly at the pictures of my children splashed across the front page. I missed them so much that my insides ached.

I wasn't raised in a churchgoing home, but I knew that God existed. I didn't know much about Him, but I did understand that He was supposed to be all-loving and merciful. The crime committed against my innocent children was so horrendous that I couldn't believe He could possibly have instigated it. Why would He want my children to die like that? Why would He want to take them away from me? Surely He didn't need them more than I did. If God was all-loving and merciful, He had to be on my side.

For the first time in my life I called out to Him. In desperation I told Him how much I hurt inside, that I felt I was nothing without my kids. "They're my whole life, God, don't You see?" I pleaded. "Bring them back, God! Please bring them back! I'm not strong enough to live without them."

Without realizing it, I had surrendered my burden to God. I was giving Him my problem and asking Him to make it right. It was the best thing I could have done.

As I sat in that dark lonely corner of my motel room a feeling of warmth filled my body. I basked in it like a fetus in the womb. A Voice spoke to me, saying, "You have not lost them. They are in My hands and I am with you. I will give you My strength to see this through."

All of a sudden it felt as if all my children were sitting on my lap! I caressed the air around them, touching and holding them. A little hand reached up to wipe away my tears. I didn't ever want to leave this corner. I had my children back.

Slowly and peacefully that feeling faded away, and I turned again to listen to the Voice. "You'll be with them again," it comforted. "You are only separated from them for a little while. The answers you seek I will show you. It has all been written down. It has all been taken care of."

When I got up from that corner I knew that God went with me. He would give me the strength to get through the children's funeral, as well as Stephanie's last days in the hospital. My Father in heaven understood the enormous loss I had sustained and would still sustain. Although I did not yet understand the full meaning of His words, I knew that somehow He had taken care of it all.

God comes to us in many ways, each according to our need and personality. Your experience will be different than mine, but He cares for every one of us. Sometimes our encounter with Him may be dramatic, but most of the time it is quiet and gentle. And we can all rest assured that He is with us.

"I will not leave you comfortless," He promises in John 14:18. "I will come to you."

"Be strong and of a good courage, fear not, nor be afraid of them: for the Lord thy God, he it is that doth go with thee; he will not fail thee, nor forsake thee" (Deuteronomy 31:6).

Are you struggling with the same emptiness that I did? Call on your heavenly Father, even if you have never spoken to Him before. Surrender your burden to Him. Tell Him, "I give up, Father. I can't bear it alone. Please help me!" And be assured, He will help! God wants so much to extend His comforting hand, to give us the strength we need to carry on. "The God of all comfort" (2 Corinthians 1:3) wants us to reach out to Him and accept the comfort He offers. He longs to answer all the questions that are tearing us apart and to wipe away our tears.

"He healeth the broken in heart, and bindeth up their wounds" (Psalm 147:3). Even God Himself recognizes that a broken heart is a wound.

Do you remember what it was like when you were a child and fell down and skinned your knee? Whom was the first person you ran to? Have you ever considered what a mother's comforting words mean to a little child?

Take a little 4-year-old, just gaining a bit of independence. He wanders up the street in pursuit of a butterfly that has caught his fancy, but the insect flitters off beyond his reach. Realizing how far away from home he has gone, he turns to run back to the safety of his own yard. In his haste, he falls on the pavement and scrapes his knee. Panic-stricken, he picks himself up and heads for home as fast as his little legs will carry him, crying as loud as he can every step of the way. Home seems to him to be miles away.

Mother hears his cries and races out to meet him.

"What happened, darling?" she calls out to him. No longer feeling big and independent, he throws himself into his mother's arms, sobbing out his whole miserable experience to her. She takes him in her arms and speaks softly and soothingly to him. All at once the tears stop. Tenderly she carries him into the house, gently washes his wound, kisses the hurt away, and places a bandage on it.

The amazing thing about this is that the little boy cried all the way home because he was trying to endure his trauma alone. But as soon as Mother held him, his tears began to dry. He trusted her, knowing that she would make it better. That confidence and trust in her gave him the strength to take the pain.

It's easy to be strong and confident and independent when life is going great. But when death stings us to the bone we begin to realize that we're still children in need of a parent to run to—someone who will wipe away the tears, kiss the hurt, and make it all better. Sometimes it takes an enormous loss to make us realize how much we still need a Savior. Close your eyes just now and tell Him it hurts so bad that you can't bear it alone. He will give you the strength to see it through.

What my dad did not realize is that God's arms were always open to him, to curl into whenever he wished and feel the security, the safety of His embrace. My dad can, if he desires, now weep until the tears won't come anymore. I know because I have also done just that.

Many of us are like my father, unable to turn to God in times of great pain. Sadly, many of us actually blame God and turn away from Him completely. The questions of why God let this happen weighs too heavy on our hearts to get past it.

But consider this: Suppose you received a phone call from your son informing you that a gang of street punks was following him and that he was scared. You'd immediately leave your house and head toward the area where your son had said he was, wouldn't you?

Now suppose that when you near the place you see four punks running down the street. Glancing into the alley, you see your son lying on the ground in a pool of blood. You run to him and lay his head on your knee, overwhelmed by what has happened. "I love you," he whispers, as he closes his eyes and breathes his last.

Noticing a knife lying beside him, you pick it up to examine the weapon that has taken his life. Just then a squad car screeches to a halt, and police officers swarm around you. One of them speaks the ominous words "You have the right to remain silent. Anything you say can and will be used against you." Incredibly, you are a suspect in the killing of your own son.

The officers slap handcuffs on your wrists and push you into the patrol car. They whisk you away like a criminal. But you didn't do it! You were there to save him, to comfort him, to bring him home. After all, you gave him life! How could they possibly suspect that you would want to take it away?

That is the way God must feel when the survivors of those who have slipped away from us falsely accuse Him. Our loved ones are His loved ones too. We are all God's children. If parents love their children, how much more does our heavenly Father, who implanted love in our hearts in the first place, feel the loss of that same child? Does such a loving Father want your loved one—His child—to die? How can we even consider such a thing!

Just as we feel the injustice of death, He experiences it too. Weeping for that which is lost, He wants to make it all right again as much as we do. And the wonderful thing is that He wants death destroyed so badly that He's already done something about it! In His infinite power and love He has indeed conquered the injustice, has righted the wrongful death of our loved ones by sacrificing His own Son for His earthly children. God doesn't want any of His children to die. He wants them to live!

"But wait," you cry out, "I just lost the most precious thing in my life! You can't really expect me to praise God right now."

Only when we understand how our loving Father is working it out for us can we begin to glorify Him. But it is not necessary to praise Him at first. He understands how we feel. In the beginning the concept of death is just too painful for anyone to be thankful for anything. So instead of praise, just pray persistently and honestly. God already knows how you feel.

He just wants you to come to Him, to share with Him, as a child does with a human father. Talk to Him just as you would to dear old dad—no formalities, just show the respect and honor due a father. With His strength you can learn to say "I shall live each day knowing that nothing could possibly happen to me that God and I can't handle together." This is my rule for living, and it has seen me through many years.

When you get up in the morning, take a moment

to ask God to help you through the day. Then talk to Him from time to time throughout it. Why try to deal with your emotions alone? Share them in private with your Father. No matter where you are— whether it be a grocery store, the office, the shower, or lying quietly in your bed—you can speak with Him (see Psalm 4:4).

Many people feel they can't converse with a God who doesn't answer back in an audible way. But if you confide in Him, seeking answers, be assured that they will come. After praying, remain quiet with your mind open. Wait for the answer of assurance that the Holy Spirit will bring to your heart. Sense His presence, His caring, His strength. Teach your children to confide in God to help them get through their day.

Another way to receive answers to prayer is to ask God to guide you to a passage of Scripture that will help you. God gave us the Bible because He wants us to know Him. He longs to have a meaningful relationship with His children. As you read your Bible, let Him open your eyes and reveal new meanings with answers to your problems. I know this works, for as I write and find I need an inspirational thought that will help someone, a verse comes to mind. Later, when I read what I have written, I am amazed at the insight God has given me.

He invites us through His Word: "Cast thy burden upon the Lord, and he shall sustain thee" (Psalm 55:22).

And remember these confident words: "I can do all things through Christ which strengtheneth me" (Philippians 4:13).

NINE

The Bigger Battle

The smell of jet fuel, mixed with the stench of burning flesh, permeated the buildings as victims fled to stairways to escape the flames. Floor by floor their numbers swelled. Strangers helped strangers, calling out to others to watch their footing in stairwells drenched by bursting pipes. Cooperation overcame the chaos, as all worked as a team in their quest to make it out alive. Calls went out to loved ones on cell phones just to say "I love you" and very possibly, "Goodbye."

They poured into the lobby by the thousands, some unsure of what to do next. Hoards of rescuers shuffled past them to reach as many as possible before flames engulfed the structures entirely.

Many victims who had been working on floors above the crash line found they had no way down. So they went up, only to be trapped on the roof of the doomed structure. With no hope of escape, many chose to end their lives quickly by plummeting 110 stories to their deaths. Steel beams, weakened by the intense heat of fuel-fed flames, collapsed like spaghetti under the strain. Onlookers watched in horror as floor after floor of the South Tower pancaked straight down, sending soot, smoke, and debris hurtling into the city streets, crushing buildings and rescuers below. Twenty-nine minutes later the North Tower went down too.

Anyone who thought the first explosion was an accident knew better when the second plane careened into the South Tower. This was not some terrible accident, but a deliberate attack on innocent lives. When word came that yet a third plane had hit the Pentagon within the same hour, America knew that it was under siege.

Emergency plans went into effect across the country. Air-traffic controllers ordered airplanes to land immediately. For the first time in history America closed all its airports. Government agencies pursued every means to find clues as to who the perpetrators might be. By nightfall we already had names of suspects and a growing case against known terrorist leader Osama bin Laden. Demands for vengeance filled the air as citizens raged in support of the nation's victims.

But another cry spread through those touched by the terror. Why did this happen to us? Why do they hate us so much that they would target the innocent? We didn't do anything to deserve this. We were just going about our daily business, not hurting anybody.

How I remember my own questions that terrible night as I, too, sought the identity of the murderers who destroyed my family in the course of just 30 minutes. Is there justice for the ones who caused all this? And are we justified in punishing them once we have evidence against them? Does that all-loving and merciful God share my rage? And if He does, why didn't He stop it from happening in the first place?

If you are searching for a reason that makes the death of your loved one seem fair or just, you will seek in vain. Death simply isn't fair!

But if you desire an answer to the cause of death and where God stands in your suffering, there is a source that gives satisfying answers. The Bible isn't the kind of book you can read from cover to cover unaided by the Holy Spirit—and expect to get answers. The solutions it contains are satisfying ones, but the individual who does not pursue them whole-heartedly will never find them.

It took me years to find answers to my questions, but God was guiding me every step along the way. When I did finally encounter the answers that satisfied my needs, they and the Spirit filled me with a peace and assurance that only truth could provide. It is peace that my father has recently come to understand, and I praise God that he finally turned to Him.

The first question that we need to address is: "Did God really want my loved one to die?" Many people blame God for death. My uncle, who seemed to be turning toward God during his daughter's battle with leukemia, made a complete about-face after she died. He said he couldn't love a God that would inflict so much pain and suffering on his little girl.

But let's think about that. If God is to blame for death, then why did He send His Son to conquer death? That would be like a firefighter who starts a fire so they can be the hero and put it out. Or a nurse who injects a patient with poison so they can administer the antidote and save the person. I would never put my children in jeopardy just to look like a hero, and neither does God.

Matthew 18:14 tells us: "It is *not* the will of your Father which is in heaven, that one of these little ones should perish."

God takes no pleasure in anyone's death, not even that of the wicked (see Ezekiel 33:11). But more than this, so intensely does God not want anyone to die that He has done something about it:

"God so loved the world, that he gave his only begotten Son, that whosoever believeth in him should not perish, but have everlasting life" (John 3:16).

Well, if God does not want us to die, why does death even exist?

The answer is that Satan brought sin into the world, and death was the result (Romans 5:12).

Long ago before the creation of humanity there existed an angel in heaven named Lucifer. He held a high and respected position in God's kingdom. But Lucifer began to question God's authority, creating doubt and unrest among the other angels. "Do we really need God to tell us what is right and wrong? After all, are we not superior beings, capable of governing ourselves without God's authority?"

Thus Lucifer started a rebellion against God, and he managed to convince fully one third of the angels to side with him (Revelation 12:4, 9). God tried to get to the root of his disaffection and appealed to him to cease his rebellion. But Lucifer spurned God's appeal. In fact, he so exalted himself that he longed to "be like the most High" (Isaiah 14:14).

Thus Lucifer became Satan. God created a perfect being, but he chose to rebel against his Maker (Ezekiel 28:15). Not satisfied with deceiving only angels, he then turned his cunning on God's newest creation, Adam and Eve (Genesis 3).

Today we live in a world in which an embittered fallen angel and his followers stalk the earth. First Peter 5:8 warns us to "be sober, be vigilant; because your adversary the devil, as a roaring lion, walketh about, seeking whom he may devour."

"We wrestle not against flesh and blood, but against principalities, against powers, against the rulers of the darkness of this world, against spiritual wickedness in high places" (Ephesians 6:12).

Sin now permeates every aspect of our society. It was not God's original plan for His children. Adam and Eve lived in a world that was fresh and clean and beautiful.

"It's all yours," God told them, spreading His arms out at the world. "Be fruitful and multiply and fill the earth. I give you dominion over it all. But please, rule it with love and be kind to My creation" (see Genesis 1:28).

We haven't done what God admonished us to do, have we? Years of human mismanagement have produced a multitude of problems. Much of humanity's suffering is self-inflicted. The tragedy is that in many instances innocent people suffer at the hands of others.

But why does God permit pain and tragedy to go on? Why didn't He just destroy Lucifer when he started his rebellion? He could have stopped sin in its tracks when it began, and we wouldn't be suffering now.

Well, believe it or not, there's a very good answer to that. If God had destroyed Lucifer just because he didn't want to bow to God's authority, wouldn't the rest of the angels have missed him and wondered what had happened? Listen to a conversation that just might have taken place if God had simply eradicated Lucifer in the beginning.

"Hey, Gabriel, whatever happened to Lucifer? I haven't seen him around lately."

"Oh, God destroyed him."

"You're kidding! Why?"

"Because Lucifer disagreed with Him."

From that point on, wouldn't the angels have obeyed God out of fear rather than love? They would have assumed that God's position was *If you don't play the game by My rules, you're history!*

No, God doesn't work that way. He gives us the freedom to decide which side we want to pledge our allegiance to. The Lord desires that we obey Him because we appreciate His character and love Him of our own free choice. Love that springs from such freedom is the only kind of love worth having. Anything else is forced, and that isn't really love. But to grant such freedom always involves risk—the risk that someone will make the wrong choice.

God wanted genuine love, so He took this risk. He permitted Lucifer to exercise his freedom of choice. By allowing Lucifer's new way of living without God's authority to have a chance, He would show the intelligent beings in His universe that Satan's way ultimately results in suffering and death—that God's way is the only way to live in peace and harmony. Because of Satan's decision to rebel, and the choice Adam and Eve made to yield to the great deceiver's temptation to eat of the forbidden fruit, "sin entered into the world, and death by sin; and so death passed upon all men" (Romans 5:12). As a result we are born sinners. And the wages of sin is death.

Now, contrary to what many believe, God does not condemn us because we were born sinners. That we could not help. He will, however—and that justly—condemn us if we reject or neglect the salvation He offers us. Here we, too, have a choice. We must decide whether to accept God's way or whether we prefer Satan's way.

Although we may not realize it, God can bring some good even out of suffering and sorrow. They can, for example, prevent us from becoming content to live our lives on earth with little desire for something far better. Death reminds us how much it hurts to lose a loved one and how precious life is. By experiencing the terrible things that sin does, we also can come to abhor sin. In fact, we can learn to hate sin so much that we yearn for its destruction and long for a life free from it.

But until God brings the reign of sin to an end, Satan will continue to inflict suffering and death upon the innocent. Meanwhile, he tries to deceive those who suffer and die—as well as those who survive them—into believing that God is to blame. He accuses our heavenly Father of the very evil for which he is responsible!

If you have any doubts, read the book of Job. Job

is our biblical example of severe loss. God inspired the book to answer some of the questions He knew we would all ask when loss strikes us. Of all the humans in the Bible, Job is the one I most look forward to meeting someday. I think we'll have much to talk about.

It's kind of a long-winded book, so I'll give you a condensed version of it.

Job was the richest, most righteous man alive—until he lost everything. Marauders stole all of his livestock, wildfires burned up his sheep, and a windstorm blew his house down and crushed all 10 of his children! On top of all this devastating loss, he developed horrible sores all over his body. The man suddenly found himself left with nothing but a pile of ashes and a very bitter wife.

"Why don't you just curse God, die, and get it over with," she asked as he sat among the ashes and scratched at his sores with a piece of broken pottery.

What kind of support did Job get from his friends? "God sure is punishing you! What did you do to deserve all this? Boy, Job, if I were you, I'd appeal to God for mercy!"

Nothing that had happened made sense to Job. "If I've done enough to deserve all this tragedy, then why are the tents of the marauders, who deserve even more, untouched?" he demanded. Nor could the ancient patriarch understand why God wouldn't answer his prayers. But Job knew he'd done nothing to deserve such tragedy.

Was God really punishing Job for his sins? No! The story tells us that Satan did it to destroy Job's loyalty to God. Sure, Job worshiped the Lord when he was rich, Satan reasoned, but would he still praise God if he lost everything vital to him? That's quite a test of faith, isn't it? Since the rebellion between God and Satan is about loyalty, God allowed Satan's attack to proceed.

Not even a righteous man like Job understood the reason for his suffering. But he endured it all and remained faithful to God, even in his questioning of God's will.

In the end, God reprimands Job's friends for accusing him of deserving such calamity, and tells Job to trust Him and to "stand up and brace yourself for battle"—a battle being fought behind the scenes and one that we can't see or fully understand.

Job's story destroys the idea that every time we suffer, it's because God is punishing us or teaching us a lesson or because we lack faith. Nobody deserved suffering less than Job, yet few in history have endured more.

Job was a wounded soldier in an unseen war. That battle still rages today. And many times we are soldiers in that war without even knowing it. We have to be strong enough, even when it hurts, to stand up and say, "Satan can hurt me, step all over me, even take away what is precious to me. But he will not defeat me, and he cannot deprive me of my salvation."

But if God is so almighty and powerful and loving, we ask, why did *my* loved one have to die? Why bother with prayers if God doesn't answer them?

The night before Stephanie died I was so angry watching her in pain that I stomped down to the hospital chapel, walked boldly to the altar, and screamed through clenched teeth, "God! You heal her now or You take her now, because she can't take any more pain!" Twelve hours later Stephanie slipped away.

Did God take her life because healing was impossible? Nothing is impossible for God. While on earth Jesus healed people and even raised them from the dead. Why couldn't He do that for Stephanie?

But then, why did God allow Satan to destroy Job's family? Because winning the bigger battle serves the greater cause right now.

More than anything on this earth, I would like to have raised my children to adulthood. But I have come to know God and where I stand in the bigger scheme of things. Before the kids were killed my desire to fight on God's side and win the bigger battle didn't even exist. I had nothing at stake that I knew of. Now I fight for my family—for God's family—because I want us to win that bigger battle—the cosmic one. I want to go home. I want my family whole!

So many people pray for healing, then lose their faith when it doesn't come. We must be assured that if we ask God, He will ultimately grant healing for those who trust Him. But for many, it will not happen until Jesus returns to earth to take us home. Yes, Jesus healed and raised the dead back to life, but those people had to wait until Jesus came to them—or they to Him. Most of us will also have to wait to see His face coming in the clouds to take us home before we receive our healing.

Occasionally God does answer prayers with miracles. But mostly He relies on us to hang in there with Him until the time is right—and only He knows when that time will be. If we could pull the curtain back so that we could see the cosmic battle raging behind the scenes, we would all agree that God has good reason to hold off. Our most heartfelt prayer should be that all of God's children will be saved—that not just our family, but God's whole family will turn to Him and be ready for His coming.

Picture it this way. If I was stranded on a ledge with all eight of my children, and a helicopter flew by and its pilot called down that he had room to rescue three of us right now, but the blast from the rotor blades would plunge the other six of us into the canyon to our deaths, would I quickly decide to save just three of us?

Now what if the pilot told me that, if we could hang on, a rescue crew could get to us in four days and we would all be saved? Would we not be willing to suffer four days with few provisions and bitter cold, for the opportunity to save us all? Yes, we would!

That's the decision God has to make, and it's one I am willing to live with to save His family, not just mine. God has not betrayed us. He has a wonderful plan of salvation beyond this world of suffering. It is not miracles but salvation that is the ultimate answer to our most heartfelt prayers.

I am ready to go home. I am ready to hold my children in my arms once again. And sometimes I grow mighty weary of the wait. But I will endure, because God has children that He wants to save. And some of them just aren't ready to go home yet.

On September 20, 2001, President George W. Bush told the nation that the "outcome is certain," and justice will prevail. As we contemplate how our nation will react to the war against terrorists in our sin-torn world, let us unite with God in the bigger battle behind the scenes. The war between good and evil will reach its climax very soon. The Bible tells us that that time is near.

TEN

Why Hast Thou Forsaken Me?

All that talk about a greater conflict between good and evil should help us to put things into perspective. Our individual existences are but fleeting moments in time in the cosmic chaos of the ages. But what if God is so concerned about the bigger battle raging in the universe that He doesn't even see the suffering we're enduring right now? Does God really understand the enormity of our agony as He looks down from heaven?

Jesus told His disciples, "If you have seen Me, you have seen the Father. How long have I been with you now and you don't know who I am?" (see John 14:9). If Jesus is exactly like the Father, then let us consider the kind of life Jesus lived while He dwelt among us and compare it to our own sufferings today. Then we must ask ourselves, Do we really have it worse than He did?

Jesus lived in an era wracked with incurable diseases, famine, poverty, and oppression. We complain about not being able to drink the water. People couldn't do it in His day, either. He spent His earliest years in exile, hiding from a wicked king who murdered every infant in Bethlehem under the age of 2—just to make sure he killed Jesus in the process.

During His life on earth Jesus and His parents suffered the snide remarks of those who taunted Him about being illegitimate. Even Nazareth, the town where He grew up, was so proverbial for its wickedness that people wondered how any good thing could ever come out of it.

When Jesus grew up He began to preach the message of His Father's love for a lost world. He came to save the world! And yet people were so much more interested in being miraculously fed and healed that they didn't seek to discover the deeper purpose of His being on earth. Jesus never owned a home or piece of land or even a donkey. Satan tempted Him, just as you and I are tempted. Yet He never sinned.

And He knew grief. The shortest verse in the Bible says that "Jesus wept" (John 11:35). He cried because His close friend Lazarus had died. Jesus was God in human flesh. His tears at Lazarus's tomb prove that God feels the pain and loss of death just as we do. Human beings are sentient creatures, created by a sensitive, feeling God.

In Lazarus's death Jesus experienced the grief of losing someone He loved just as we suffer grief. But even more, Jesus endured the grief of knowing that although He had come to offer human beings eternal life, few seemed willing to accept His inestimable gift or appreciate the sacrifice He would make on Calvary.

Those He loved eventually betrayed and denied Him. He was mocked and scourged, beaten and spat upon by those He came to save. Yet through it all He pitied their wretched souls.

He felt the enormity of His loneliness on the night before His crucifixion as He knelt in Gethsemane and bared His soul to the sword of justice. Three times He sought consolation from His friends, and three times He found them asleep, oblivious to the mental anguish He was going through. Haven't we all felt that lonely anguish—of needing a friend so badly and finding nobody to turn to?

Jesus did nothing to deserve execution. Yet He received the most horrible death humanity can inflict upon a person. Nails tore into His flesh through tendon, muscle, and nerves and out the other side. I think of the bullets ripping through my children's bodies, and I know my Savior understands their pain.

Crucifixion was deliberately intended to be a slow and agonizing way to die. It could take days. Because they wouldn't leave a prisoner hanging over the Sabbath, the local religious authorities had the Romans pierce His side to hasten His death, just as my 3-year-old daughter was stabbed with a steak knife—and again I know my Savior understands.

As I think of the excruciating pain, the mental cries for help my children must have silently screamed, and I remember my Savior hanging on the cross, pleading to his Father, "Why hast thou forsaken me?" I know my Savior understands. I serve a God who has felt my anguish—a God who also suffered for me and my loved ones.

Second Corinthians 1:3-5 declares: "Praise be to the God and Father of our Lord Jesus Christ, the Father of compassion and the God of all comfort, who comforts us in all our troubles, so that we can comfort those in any trouble with the comfort we ourselves have received from God. For just as the sufferings of Christ flow over into our lives, so also through Christ our comfort overflows" (NIV).

When one of our own dies, God cries too. The Bible says that "precious in the sight of the Lord is the death of his saints" (Psalm 116:15). Having experienced what it is to lose a Son by death, He is able to comfort us when we suffer loss. He is "the God of all comfort; who comforteth us in all our tribulation" (2 Corinthians 1:3, 4).

If we must then endure suffering in this world, what lies beyond it? What do we have to look forward to? Scripture declares: "Now for a little while you may have had to suffer grief in all kinds of trials. These have come so that your faith . . . may be proved genuine and may result in praise, glory and honor when Jesus Christ is revealed" (1 Peter 1:6, 7).

During His sojourn on earth Jesus constantly spoke of His Father's kingdom. He wants us to look beyond the present life of pain toward a new life with Him. But sometimes grief does strange things to the mind. Even Jesus, as He hung on the cross, cried out in despair, "My God, why hast thou forsaken me?" (Mark 15:34).

In your grief, have you felt separated from God? Has the outlook been so gloomy that you could not see any hope?

I would like to share a thought with you. Psalm 23:4 says: "Yea, though I walk through the valley of the shadow of death, I will fear no evil: for thou art with me." The psalm depicts death here as a deep valley—so deep, in fact, that we feel desperately alone and desolate as we journey through it. But we are not alone. We notice a shadow cast before us. Have you ever seen a shadow without a light to produce it? Of course you haven't. If there is a shadow, then there must be light—Jesus, "the light of the world." Although we may not discern his presence, He is with us.

Our God does not want us to suffer and hurt alone. He reaches down His comforting hand to give us hope, love, assurance, and the strength to travel through that valley. God desires to answer all the questions that haunt us night and day. The Lord longs to wipe away all tears from our eyes—and someday He will, when He finally destroys sin and Satan (see Revelation 7:17; 21:4).

Even though Jesus felt that God had forsaken Him as He hung on the cross, angels invisible to human eyes surrounded Him, wanting desperately to reach down and relieve His suffering. But they knew that if they did, it would shatter the plan of salvation and cause the loss of humanity forever. Thus Satan and his lawless way of life must have seemed to triumph.

When Jesus breathed His last upon the cross, He cried out, "It is finished" (John 19:30), and those who loved Him wept bitter tears. As they gathered to comfort one another, many wondered if they hadn't made a mistake in believing that He was the Messiah. Now He lay dead, shattering all their hopes. But on the morning of the third day God restored His Son to life, and Jesus rose from His tomb triumphant over death. At that moment He won the victory over death.

Days later, when Jesus ascended to heaven, the disciples again felt deep sorrow as they watched Him disappear from sight. To comfort them God sent two angels who declared, "Ye men of Galilee, why stand ye gazing up into heaven? This same Jesus, which is taken up from you into heaven, shall so come in like manner as ye have seen him go into heaven" (Acts 1:11). Jesus is coming again! Does this seem too good to be true?

"I go to prepare a place for you," Jesus promised. "And if I go and prepare a place for you, *I will come again,* and receive you unto myself; that where I am, there ye may be also" (John 14:2, 3).

"Marvel not at this: for the hour is coming, in the which all that are in the graves shall hear his voice, and shall come forth" (John 5:28, 29).

"The Lord himself shall descend from heaven with a shout, with the voice of the archangel, and with the trump of God: and the dead in Christ shall rise first: then we which are alive and remain shall be caught up together with them in the clouds, to meet the Lord in the air: and so shall we ever be with the Lord. Wherefore comfort one another with these words" (1 Thessalonians 4:16-18).

"God shall wipe away all tears from their eyes; and there shall be no more death, neither sorrow, nor crying, neither shall there be any more pain: for the former things are passed away" (Revelation 21:4).

With such words of assurance, I can hardly wait

to be with my loved ones again! But I will be patient, knowing that I shall one day soon see them again. Meanwhile I look "for that blessed hope, and the glorious appearing of the great God and our Saviour Jesus Christ" (Titus 2:13).

Pain and suffering are a part of life on our planet, and no one is exempt. Faith in God does not place us in a bubble, impenetrable by germs, disease, bullets, or speeding cars. Christians suffer just like everybody else. Jesus continually warned us that the world would persecute us. Satan will seek to destroy our loyalty to God. But if we remain faithful, especially in our trials, we won't be disappointed when we see our greatest hopes fulfilled.

The Bible says: "We also rejoice in our sufferings, because we know that suffering produces perseverance; perseverance, character; and character, hope. And hope does not disappoint us" (Romans 5:3-5, NIV).

ELEVEN

Vengeance Is Mine

I did not go to the police station of my own accord. I would have stayed outside my house all night. They could refuse to let me in, but sooner or later they'd have to bring the bodies out. Only then could I believe it really happened—that my children were really dead. But I had no choice about the matter.

Immediately upon our arrival at the police station, officers took my husband to an interrogation room, leaving me alone with a minister for four hours in a front office. In those hours my rage intensified. How could someone just walk into my house and shoot my children? Why couldn't I find the ones who did it, string them up, and shoot them a thousand times? Doesn't the Bible say "an eye for an eye"? I wanted justice. I wanted revenge! And I wanted it now.

But the minister didn't agree with me. "You should feel sorry for the ones who did this to your children."

"Why should I feel sorry for them?" I demanded. "They're murderers!"

A lot of time has passed since that intensely angry night. Time to ponder the minister's response to my rage. Time to ask God how He feels about what happened to the children and how He regards the killers. And time to ask God what he expects of me.

The Bible teaches us to pray: "Forgive us our debts, as we forgive our debtors. . . . For if ye forgive men their trespasses, your heavenly Father will also forgive you: but if ye forgive not men their trespasses, neither will your Father forgive your trespasses" (Matthew 6:12-15).

I hated the passage the first time I read it, because it demanded something of me that I could not do. I could forgive life's usual injustices, but God couldn't possibly expect me to forgive murderers. My human need for vindication told me that, whether they ever showed remorse or not, the murderers had no right to live after taking innocent lives. Was it wrong for me to feel this way?

I recognize that this is a complex issue with many perspectives and viewpoints. But I believe that we always need to keep the following points in mind.

The Bible contains many passages about forgiving, and they can really get you to thinking about how God wants us to feel about our fellow human beings here on earth. The forgiveness issue is a valid one, and I don't want anybody to think that what I'm about to present to you is permission to do whatever you want to anybody. The Bible tells us "as ye would that men should do to you, do ye also to them likewise" (Luke 6:31) and "thou shalt love thy neighbour as thyself" (Leviticus 19:18; cf. Matthew 19:19; 22:39; Mark 12:31).

But murder is, I believe, an entirely different subject, and even God Himself has no tolerance for it. After Noah and his family left the ark, God told Noah to repopulate the earth again. He also said that Noah could kill animals for food. In the next breath He informed Noah that "whoso sheddeth man's blood, by man shall his blood be shed: for in the image of God made he man" (Genesis 9:6).

After Moses led God's people through the wilderness for 40 years, they came at last to the Promised Land. Under God's instruction, Moses wrote down the laws that His people were to observe. In chapters in two books (Numbers 35 and Deuteronomy 19) God commanded them to build six cities of refuge so that every innocent "slayer" could flee to the nearest one. He gave us an example of such an individual. If two men went out to chop firewood, and the head of the first one's axe accidentally flew off and killed his neighbor, the "slayer" was to flee at once to the city of refuge before the "blood avenger"—the person who sought justice for the victim's family—had a chance to catch up with him. Should he make it through the gates before the victim's family captured him, the city would provide refuge for him for the rest of his life.

But if a man hated his neighbor and with premeditation killed him, then fled to the city of refuge, he could not remain there. The community leaders had to return him to the blood avenger. Numbers 35:18, 19 declared that if a person willfully killed another, "he is a murderer: the murderer shall surely be put to death. The revenger of blood himself shall slay the murderer." The avenger was to have no regret for doing what God commanded him to do. "Thine eye shall not pity; but life shall go for life, eye for eye, tooth for tooth, hand for hand, foot for foot" (Deuteronomy 19:21). "So these things shall be for a statute of judgment unto you throughout your generations in all your dwellings" (Numbers 35:29).

Some argue that such Old Testament laws applied just to Israel and that Jesus is kinder and gentler than His Father. That He expects us to turn the other cheek. But when Jesus walked the earth, the Old Testament was all that existed. Every time He said "It is written" He was quoting the Old Testament. Deuteronomy was one of the books Jesus and His disciples most often quoted. The New Testament has more than 80 references to Deuteronomy. Why would Jesus cite it so many times if He planned to completely do away with it?

God never changes. Not only does He demand that the punishment fit the crime in order to maintain an orderly society, He fully expects that punishment to be meted out to those who are guilty.

So what about that whole "turn the other cheek" business Jesus preached about?

In Luke 6 Jesus teaches tolerance in an intolerant world. He's telling us to love our enemies, do good to those who hate us, pray for those who spitefully use us. They are some of the most beautiful words of advice Jesus ever gave us, and we should all follow them. But they are not speaking about the problem of murder.

The "eye for an eye" advice that God gave us does, however, deal with the issue of retribution, of the need to find a balanced justice in society. If someone stole from you, the law limited retribution to the value of replacing the item lost. The offending party was then forgiven and the offended party commanded to restrain from seeking further retribution. Without such laws it was not uncommon for the offended party to take retribution out on the offender's entire family, and the punishment was far more severe than the crime.

If you look at it as a way to control the social advantage of the rich of that day, you begin to see that God is truly a God of justice. The punishment was to fit the crime—"an eye for an eye"—and He clearly states that the punishment for death is death—not for the perpetrator's whole family, but certainly for the perpetrator.

God implanted in each human heart a sense of justice and fairness. It is a reflection of His own character, part of the image of God within us (see Genesis 1:27). Life is infinitely valuable, because it comes from God. He does not want us to take its loss lightly. And most of us don't. When someone dies from any cause, it causes great grief and heartache. And when someone deliberately kills another, the pain is perhaps even worse.

When tragedy strikes, we want what happens to us to be taken seriously—and God does. Taking a life is the most terrible thing we can do to another person—and God understands the anguish and horror of the victim's loved ones and friends. We must not dismiss premeditated murder as something that can be easily forgiven. And this applies to the terrorist attacks. This was not a declared war between armies but an attack on citizens. If we did not react in horror of senseless acts, something would be wrong with us. Our consciences and feelings would be seared.

Thousands died in the World Trade Center and the Pentagon. The terrorists lay in wait and then killed with hatred and premeditation. It is my hope that our nation will find a way to bring the terrorists to justice. This was not a war over boundaries or political powers or a battle between soldier and soldier. This can only be considered murder, and we must recognize the seriousness of what has happened and the impact it has on the public as a whole. As I watch nations unite as a single force to root out these criminals, I cannot help recognizing the importance of their mission. The task that lies ahead of us is a daunting one. Our enemy promises to be a formidable opponent. But our responsibility is to punish the guilty and protect the innocent. It is a good sign that many defend the American Islamic community both in act and word, reminding us that only those who "lie in wait" should be punished. Let us truly be "one nation under God, indivisible, with liberty and justice for all"—liberty for the innocent and justice for the guilty and their victims.

May all our victims be vindicated, for that is a part of the healing process, too.

TWELVE

Widening Our Coping Range

We'd been told to board the plane as quickly as possible. It would be a full flight to Minneapolis. The luck of the draw had been against me this time, however. I was in the second-to-the-last row of the plane.

"Oh, well, we can't all sit in 7-C," I reasoned as I adjusted my seat belt and prepared for takeoff.

Seconds before our scheduled departure time, an elderly couple boarded in a frazzle and searched the aisles for their assigned seat numbers. When they realized that the airline had placed them in the very *last* row of the plane, their jaws dropped and both flew into hysterics.

"This is totally unacceptable!" the man complained to the flight attendant. "We were promised a window seat!"

I glanced back to see what the commotion was all about. Their "window seat" had no window because the plane's engines were mounted just outside on the fuselage. The flight attendant apologized but pointed out that there were no other available seats. The couple glared at her as if her answer was equally unacceptable. Surely she would reseat them, even if someone else had to sit there. But she did not.

Throughout the flight the two made sure everyone around them knew they were *not* happy flyers. The man strained to see out other windows, ignoring the passengers he disturbed in his efforts.

"This is absurd," he whined, squirming in his seat like a toddler.

At the same time he pushed against my backrest until I wanted to turn around and knock some sense into him. As if the seats weren't bad enough for them, the couple informed the attendant that the snack was inedible and the plane was too warm. Even as we were gathering our luggage to disembark, the two were still at it.

I shook my head in disgust as the pair brushed past me. "I hope this is the worst thing that happens to you today," I whispered after them. "I've seen days that this one wouldn't hold a candle to."

When I returned the following week, bad weather in Minneapolis delayed my flight in St. Louis. I had to accept the fact that I might very well miss my connecting flight home. Since I own no credit cards, the delay would mean I would most likely be spending the night in the Minneapolis Airport—and I had checked my luggage.

Well, I thought, *worse things could happen. At least the airport will be warm. I have $5 to buy a few snacks, and I've slept sitting up a time or two before. If it's the worst* *thing that happens to me today, I can handle it.*

We took off two hours after the scheduled departure, too late to make my connecting flight, I was sure. But I was in good company on the plane. At least I'd be this much closer to home, I reasoned, and they'd get me on the first flight home that had room for me.

As we neared Minneapolis the attendant announced which connecting flights had already departed. Mine was still circling Minneapolis, waiting to land, so there was hope.

A half hour later I jumped off the plane and ran for the desk. A covey of frazzled flyers hovered there, calling out their destinations for departure gates. Fargo, North Dakota—not a chance. Sioux Falls—already gone.

"Billings, Montana," I shouted.

The attendant scanned the list of gates. "Run!" she yelled to me. "As fast as you can to Gate 76. They're pulling away from the gate right now."

I took off as if my feet were on fire and made it to the gate as they were locking the door. Panting and puffing, I hurried down the aisle, looking for my seat assignment . . . and there it was—the *last row,* the very same windowless seat the older couple had gone into convulsions over more than a week before.

"Praise the Lord for this seat," I said to myself as I slid into the dark little corner. "I'm on the plane, and I'm going home!" Nothing would dampen my joy. I didn't have to see where I was going to get there.

As we pulled away from the gate the thought struck me that my luggage was *not* going to make my plane. It had had no time to get off the other plane and onto this one. *Oh well,* I thought, *I can make do with what's at home till the luggage arrives. At least I'll be home!*

I landed in Billings at midnight, and my husband and children greeted me with exuberant hugs. At the baggage claim I wasn't surprised when my luggage didn't appear on the carousel. The baggage handler was telling a man in front of us that it would be to-morrow night before the luggage arrived. The trav-eler flew into a rage.

"Tomorrow night!" he bellowed. "Do you know what this is going to cost me?"

I thought about what that might mean. Did he have a big business deal? Was he implying that he'd have to buy a bunch of clothes and toiletries to get by?

Shaking his fist at the baggage handler, he scolded, "This is going to cost me a whole day of my vacation!"

I had to hold myself back from laughing. Some of us are too busy surviving day-to-day to afford vaca-tions! I walked away from the man, chanting the words inside me: "I hope this is the worst thing that happens to you today!"

My luggage arrived two days later after being ac-cidentally rerouted. I had to wear my Carhartt over-alls and use my old toothbrush. I employed the delay as an opportunity to do a lot of yard work and clean out the barn.

I saw no need to go into fits over the situation. Nothing had purposely targeted me—or any other passenger on board—for all the inconvenience. It was purely circumstance that things happened the way they did. If we can't handle the ordinary circumstances in our lives, we'll never withstand the truly tragic things that undoubtedly will come our way.

AVERAGE COPING RANGE

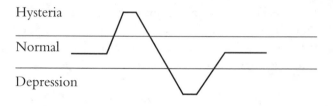

The chart above gives us an example of how most people cope with life's ups and downs. The center margin represents normal daily activities and our emotional reaction to them. As long as life treats us fairly our emotions remain stable. We're on an even keel sailing along in calm seas . . . until *Boom!* Tragedy strikes.

It sends us up into the storm clouds of hysteria, where the winds of adversity toss and batter us until we finally plunge into the sea of deep despair. Here we remain until, one day, we look up and decide we don't want to be down here anymore. We want to climb back up to normal again.

Widening our coping range broadens what we can endure—how much wind our sails can take before we get pushed off course. It gives us the resilience we need to look on the bright side of each situation, or at least to put it into proper perspective. If we widen our coping ranges *before* tragedy strikes, we'll find it easier to withstand the trials that follow. But it's never too late to start.

Coping range has nothing to do with physical

strength or size. All three of my fellow passengers were larger than I am. It does, however, have everything to do with our individual characters—our inner strengths and weaknesses. Those of us who have had to face adversity in life learn that it is something we must deal with. We can either choose to let the situation defeat us, or we can decide to rise above it.

Put yourself in the story above. How would you have coped with a similar situation? If you see yourself reacting more like my fellow passengers, perhaps its time for you to explore ways to widen your coping range as well. So where do we begin?

If we make a list of our own personal strengths and weaknesses, we can gain a clearer view of whom we really are. Then we can focus on just how we can strengthen ourselves against life's adversities.

As you compare the list of strengths and weaknesses below, circle the number that best describes you in most situations. For example, if you feel that you have the determination to accept challenges as they come without flinching, circle number 4. If you tend to shy away from challenges, circle 1. Or if you see yourself not quite at either extreme, choose 3 or 2, whichever tendency you lean toward.

Do you have a temper that you find is often hard to get a handle on, or do you control a righteous anger? I admit I had to get help from God on that one. Yes, it is possible for God to turn hatred and vengeance into righteous anger—even when you have a choleric personality. That's what we all need to strive for in the current situation that America is in right now.

Go ahead and circle the strength or weakness that best describes you.

STRENGTH   weakness

Determination	4 3 2 1	Withdraw From Challenge
Righteous Anger	4 3 2 1	Uncontrolled Temper
Born Fighter	4 3 2 1	No Will to Live
Deep Concern for Others	4 3 2 1	Uncaring/Self-preserving
Hobbies	4 3 2 1	Few Recreational Interests
Special Talents	4 3 2 1	Can Barely Tie My Own Shoes
Faith in a Higher Being	4 3 2 1	No Faith at All
Assertive	4 3 2 1	Wimp
Helpful to Others	4 3 2 1	Helpless
Imaginative/Creative	4 3 2 1	Lack Vision
Good Listener	4 3 2 1	Poor Listener
Articulate	4 3 2 1	Too Shy to Speak Up
Studious (Eager to Learn)	4 3 2 1	Know It All Already
Understanding	4 3 2 1	Bullheaded
Good Health	4 3 2 1	Poor Health
Exercise Regularly	4 3 2 1	Couch Potato
Balanced Diet	4 3 2 1	Junk Food Junkie
Sense of Humor	4 3 2 1	Can't Take a Joke
Grateful	4 3 2 1	Grumbler
Enjoy Your Occupation	4 3 2 1	Hate Your Job
High Self-esteem	4 3 2 1	Dirt Has More Value
Good Marriage	4 3 2 1	Take My Spouse, Please!
Strong Friendships	4 3 2 1	Nobody Likes Me
Optimist	4 3 2 1	Pessimist

Don't be too discouraged by the results. We all have our strengths as well as our weak areas to work on. As you study your own weaknesses, try to think of ways to change them into strengths. For instance, do you need to listen more to others to overcome your bullheadedness? Is it time to take a good look at your diet, your activities, your job? Will counseling help turn things around for you now that you know what areas in your life need help? Ask a loved one to help you strengthen those weak spots by testing you with examples, or reminding you in a loving way when your efforts fail.

One of the weaknesses I noticed most in myself was that I don't know how to ask for help. I've been working on it at home and at work, and my everyday burden has gotten easier. I used to think it was a weakness to need assistance. Now, I know it's a strength to be able to ask others to lighten my load, and I've learned that people love me enough to want to do it for me.

As you begin to strengthen your weaknesses, your coping range begins to widen. You will feel more confident about yourself and your ability to see things through. When you do find yourself in a sticky situation, step back and assess your options first. Decide just how bad the situation really is, and try to see the bright side of it: I have no window, but I'm going home. If I hadn't made the plane, at least the airport was warm, well lit, and had food and security guards. It beats the streets, right?

The best way to widen our coping range is to take care of the four basic areas of our lives—our physical, mental, social, and spiritual selves—so that we have a built-in support system even when we are alone. The prospect of sleeping in a strange airport far from home seemed bearable because I have built up my spiritual support system to sustain me through the tough times. I am never alone, because God is with me. And if God is with me, I don't have reason to be afraid of any situation. That doesn't mean I go out and court trouble, though! Nor does being mentally strong mean I'm invincible.

Now look at our new coping range chart.

OUR NEW WIDENED COPING RANGE

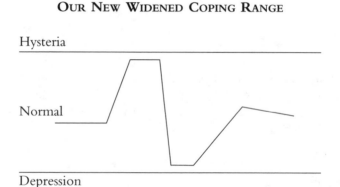

Hysteria

Normal

Depression

By widening our coping range, we bring all those things that fling people up into hysteria or down into depression within our normal ability to cope. We can stay on course without extreme emotion or inconvenience. Many things in life may not be the way we would choose them to be, but we can cope with them. All of us are capable of becoming stronger individuals. But it does take some effort to get there.

POSITIVE WAYS TO EASE THE PAIN

Once we expand our coping range, we can explore ways to make our adjustment after loss easier or more comfortable. That doesn't mean we will be healed in a matter of months. It's going to take years to heal fully from such a tragic loss. Even years later, we may need to find ways to turn the pain into something positive or productive. Days are still going to come that will test our coping ability. Birthdays, holidays, and anniversaries especially challenge our strengths and brutalize our weaknesses. September 11 will be a haunting day for America for a long time to come. But what can we do to turn bitter remorse into beautiful tributes?

I had to come to grips with this when the calendar confronted me with a birthday for which I was not ready. On September 27, 1991, my daughter Tonya should have turned 18 years old. I was not emotionally ready to accept that this child, had she lived, would be grown up already. I had lost too many years to let her go, even in my mind.

As a result I moped about the house, fretting and wondering what I could do about it. I had to do something to make the day special in memory of Tonya. I thought about what I might have done had she lived to see this day. A mother-daughter luncheon to honor her entry into womanhood? Yes, that's what we would have done. Could I still do it anyway? Yes, I could. The Lord had blessed me with one daughter following the loss of my other three. Sandy was now 13, a threshold year all in its own for a girl. She too would soon slip away from me to seek her own fu-

ture. I could honor Tonya by honoring the relationship that all mothers and daughters share.

I called three friends, each with one daughter, and
invited them to a mother-daughter appreciation dinner at a local café. We were all "4-H Fence Moms"—
mothers who spent the entire summer sitting on the
arena fence at the fairgrounds, cheering our daughters
on in horse shows, clinics, and gymkhanas, and con-
fiding among ourselves about how our teenage
daughters didn't appreciate our sacrifice and wisdom.
This dinner would be our chance to show our appreciation for each other.

I dug out my late mother-in-law's lacy wedding
tablecloth and took it down to the café. The tablecloth represented the continuity of the family and
honored the generations that come and go beyond us.
Then I bought yellow mini-corsages for all eight of us
in Tonya's honor, because yellow was her favorite
color. Finding poems about mothers and daughters in
old Mother's Day cards and poetry books, I printed
them on pastel paper and sealed them with fancy
stickers from Hallmark. One of the daughters is blind,
so I took her poem to the high school, where her
teacher helped her print it in braille.

We had a wonderful meal. Afterward we each
read our poems aloud—mothers about daughters, and
daughters about mothers. Tears flowed freely among
the mothers, and the daughters used the occasion to
thank their moms for being so special.

I said goodbye to Tonya that day in a way I never
had before. Now I can look back on her birthday
with fond memories.

We can do lots of things to honor our loved ones in a positive way. When a special day comes that's hard for you, buy yourself flowers or a corsage in the individual's memory. I wore my yellow mini-corsage for three days until it shriveled up. I even took it to a horse show with my jeans and cowboy hat. It made me the proudest mom on the fence that day.

Early on, my husband and I decided that each of our children would have flowers in their favorite color. The florist knows all about our pink, yellow, orange, blue, and purple carnations. If I want to do something in the kids' memory, these colors always play a part. Go someplace you and your loved one used to enjoy, or even a spot you always dreamed of visiting together but never got around to it. Invite a friend to join you and enjoy it with all the gusto you can give it. When you get home and climb into bed, you'll feel satisfaction instead of emptiness.

Let's look beyond ourselves and our loss now. There are so many things we can do to help others in our loved one's name that I can't possibly list them all. It can be as simple as donating a book to the library in the lost one's name. Choose a subject that was important to the loved one. Take coloring books or games to a children's hospital in your child's name. Sponsor a Little League team or donate equipment.

Our son Steve's employers thought so much of him that they collected money to buy a memorial showcase to display science projects at the junior high school. His favorite subject was biology. Seventeen years later I visited the school. The showcase is still there. Today it houses art projects, an equally fitting purpose for it.

Maybe you can afford to do something bigger. People have established memorial grants, scholarships, and whole foundations to help others fulfill goals that were important to their loved one. Think of a dream or a passion that your loved one had and use it to spark ideas.

Doing something positive helps determine whether we will look back on our losses with comfort or with regret. While we will never fully escape the hurt, our loved ones would want us to be happy, productive, secure human beings. We owe it to their memory to strive to be stronger for the loss. In comparison to losing them, everything else in life should be easier.

THIRTEEN

Personal Reflections

The year after our children were killed Barbara Mandrell sang a popular song about faded photographs bringing back feelings about someone we still loved. We were driving into the cemetery the first time I heard the song, and it amazed me that the singer knew exactly how I felt. The years that have passed since I first heard it have not taken away the poignancy of those words.

We spent a lot of time at the cemetery that first year. To us, the cemetery was a place we could bring our family back together. It's a beautiful spot, full of trees and well-groomed lawns. The children had become so much a part of our lives that George and I couldn't imagine making plans for the future without them. Only after I became pregnant did we realize we had to start living again. After the birth of our daughter Sandy our feelings of joy mixed with sorrow that she would never know her brothers and sisters.

Sandy learned to walk on the green cemetery lawns. She fed the ducks that swam on the cemetery lake and sniffed the flowers that polka-dotted the grounds. Toddling about in the giant mausoleum in which George's grandparents were laid to rest, she couldn't resist screaming in her high-pitched voice after she learned that it would echo in the massive marble building. Back in those days we would spend hours out there together, as naturally as any other family getting together for a picnic.

Living more than 1,000 miles from the cemetery now, we don't get there very often. But we never pass up a chance to go whenever we're close enough. A couple visits have been en route to a new home, encumbered by a fully loaded Ryder truck and a trailerful of horses. But this has not diminished the reverence we show when we visit.

Just as God blessed Job with more children, George and I have been blessed with three beautiful, healthy children since the tragedy. There was never a time when we sat the children down and told them what happened to their brothers and sisters. It is as if they have always known.

When we go to the cemetery Sandy, Matthew, and Michael know that this is where their brothers and sisters are. Although they never knew them, yet they have lived their entire lives in their shadows. They've grown up with stories of their siblings, their grandparents, and all the other relatives that passed before them. Thus they feel a heritage behind them, a continuity in something that started long before them and will continue long after they are gone. The children know they will never be forgotten in a family like ours.

Matthew has shown the most sensitivity. When

he was small he would sometimes break out crying for no apparent reason. When I would take him aside to comfort him, he'd tell me he was crying for his brothers and sisters. We'd cry together, but we are comforted by the promise that Jesus will come to make it all right some day.

Through the years we've had to address the feelings of vengeance that each of the children have felt. It's been necessary to talk out what happened and what kind of justice they would administer if it were their job. Michael's justice would be to smear the children's killers with honey and tie them over a fire ant hill. Matthew prefers the slow, painful justice of a bow and arrow. It may sound gruesome to many, but those who have lost a loved one by the hand of another will understand those feelings and the need for expressing and coming to terms with them.

George and I now have very little contact with anyone who knew our children. Sometimes this is difficult for us. But we cling to the memories we both share and the love that binds those memories together. I am fortunate in that I am blessed with a husband with whom I can share all my thoughts. Without a doubt, aside from Christ the most important thing that George and I have is each other. The loss has made our family all the more precious, and nobody leaves the house or the phone without saying "I love you," just in case it is our last opportunity.

We have raised our three living children to carry on the family name and the pride it stands for. I feel great satisfaction in the fine young people they have come to be. And I know they are ready for the challenges that face them in this world. They have an incredible sense of justice, and both of our boys have expressed their conviction that—if their country calls on them to bring the terrorists to justice—they will go and fight valiantly for the cause. I fear for my sons, as any mother would, but I am proud that the issue is that important to them.

My three living children have taught me that it is possible to love someone you have never met. It is possible to feel the injustice of a life that was lost without your ever experiencing a day of it. And it is possible to long for a restoration of something you never experienced. This has helped me in my mission to feel compassion for all who have lost.

During the past several years I have devoted my time to reaching out to others who may be grieving across the country. I have turned my tragedy into a way to help those who need hope beyond this world of pain. The stories I am told would break your heart. Does this depress me? No. It affirms that my mission has purpose. It reminds me that I am not alone in my own losses—that I am one among a vast community of wounded soldiers. And it sustains the hope that burns deep inside that I will one day hold my loved ones again. Yet no matter how many places I go, there are so many more I have not reached.

I wish I could wrap my arms around each and every one of the survivors of September 11, 2001—to offer my shoulder to cry on and a listening ear. I wish I could help each of them to understand that the pain will eventually fade and that there are people out there who really care.

Everyone who loses a loved one receives many different cards of sympathy. It amazes me as I look through all the cards we received, just how many of them say something to this effect:

"Words cannot express our sorrow." "Although we cannot know exactly how you feel, we hope that just knowing there are so many who care will help to comfort you." "What does one say at a time like this?"

Such expressions help me realize that when death strikes, the feelings that friends have are pretty universal. They really don't know what to say, and we see this lack often reflected in the cards they send.

But one card we received carried a message in it that I was able to cling to. Perhaps you too can find strength in it, to help carry you through your own time of grief.

If I can endure for this moment
Whatever is happening to me,
No matter how heavy my heart is
Or how "dark" the moment may be—
If I can remain calm and quiet
With all my world crashing about me,
Secure in the knowledge God loves me
When everyone else seems to doubt me—
If I can but keep on believing
What I know in my heart to be true,
That "Darkness will fade in the morning"
And that this will pass away, too—
Then nothing in life can defeat me
For as long as this knowledge remains
I can suffer whatever is happening
For I know God will break "all the chains"
That are binding me tight in "The Darkness"
And trying to fill me with fear—
For there is "No Night Without Dawning"
And I know that "My Morning" is near.

—Helen Steiner Rice